SHOE LA

CHECK FOR THE
RETURN.

eros

ral
as
s

EAST OF MÁLAGA

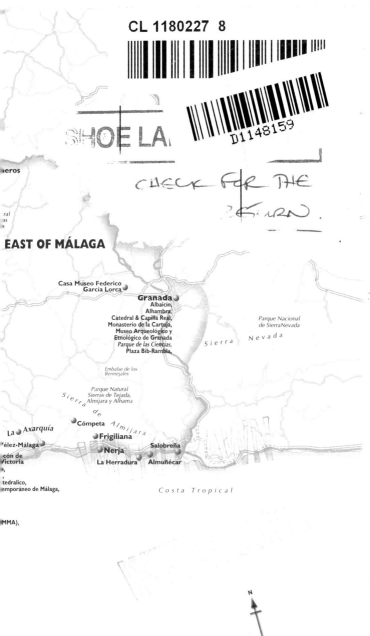

Casa Museo Federico
García Lorca

Granada
Albaicín,
Alhambra,
Catedral & Capilla Real,
Monasterio de la Cartuja,
Museo Arqueológico y
Etnológico de Granada
Parque de las Ciencias,
Plaza Bib-Rambla,

*Parque Nacional
de SierraNevada*

Sierra   Nevada

*Embalse de los
Bermejales*

*Parque Natural
Sierras de Tejada,
Almijara y Alhama*

Sierra   de   Almijara

La Axarquía   **Cómpeta**

Frigiliana

élez-Málaga   **Nerja**   Salobreña
cón de   La Herradura   Almuñécar
Victoria

tedralico,
emporáneo de Málaga,   *Costa   Tropical*

MMA),

N
↑

TWINPACK
Costa del Sol

MARY-ANN GALLAGHER

If you have any comments
or suggestions for this guide
you can contact the editor at
Twinpacks@theAA.com

AA Publishing
Find out more about AA Publishing and the wide
range of services the AA provides by visiting our
website at theAA.com/bookshop

How to Use This Book

This guide is divided into four sections

• Essential Costa del Sol: An introduction to the region and tips on making the most of your stay.

• Costa del Sol by Area: We've broken the region into three areas, and recommended the best sights, shops, activities, restaurants, entertainment and nightlife venues in each one. Suggested walks and drives help you to explore.

• Where to Stay: The best hotels, whether you're looking for luxury, budget or something in between.

• Need to Know: The info you need to make your trip run smoothly, including getting about by public transport, weather tips, emergency phone numbers and useful websites.

Navigation In the Costa del Sol by Area chapter, we've given each area its own colour, which is also used on the locator maps throughout the book and the map on the inside front cover.

Maps The fold-out map accompanying this book is a comprehensive map of the Costa del Sol. The grid on this fold-out map is the same as the grid on the locator maps within the book. The grid references to these maps are shown with capital letters, for example A1. The grid references to the town plan are shown with lower-case letters, for example a1.

Contents

CONTENTS

Introducing the Costa del Sol

The Costa del Sol, a glittering swathe of the Mediterranean coast, enjoys a year-round balmy climate and magnificent beaches. But beyond sun, sea and sand there are stylish cities, fun-filled resorts, remote villages and rugged mountains.

It's hard to believe that only a few decades ago the Costa del Sol was a largely untouched region scattered with fishing villages. Now it boasts some of the most celebrated resorts in Spain, from the hedonistic delights of Torremolinos and Fuengirola to the exclusive enclave of Puerto Banús. The glorious beaches are well-maintained and endowed with every facility, with excellent amenities for watersports and other outdoor activities.

Málaga, the capital of the Costa del Sol, has long been overlooked in the charge for the beaches, but this engaging and vibrant city is beginning to entice increasing numbers of visitors thanks to the success of the excellent Museo Picasso which opened in 2003. The city's alluring *casco antiguo* (old quarter) is dominated by the lofty remains of a great Arabic fortress, the Alcazaba, which offers stunning views.

Officially, the Costa del Sol extends along the Malagueño coastline, from Nerja in the northeast to Estepona in the south. However, this book also covers the enticing inland regions and includes the great triumverate of Andalucian cities: Granada, Sevilla (Seville) and Córdoba. Thanks to excellent road and rail links, all three cities are easily accessible from Málaga and most of the coastal resorts.

Inland is a very different story from the cosmopolitan coastline. The mountainous hinterland is scattered with lofty white villages spilling down the hillsides, and tranquil valleys are filled with olive groves and fruit orchards. Many areas are preserved as natural parks, and provide excellent opportunities for hiking, bird-watching and adventure activities. Public transport is limited, however, and a car is essential to really get off the beaten track or into the mountains.

Facts + Figures

- **Average number of sunny days a year on the Costa del Sol: 320**
- **Average temperature: 22ºC (72ºF)**
- **Average sea temperatures: January 15º (59ºF); August 24ºC (75ºF)**

ANTONIO BANDERAS

Picasso may be Málaga's most famous son—but not by much. Antonio Banderas remains enormously popular in his home town of Málaga. He is still very involved in the Spanish cinema scene, despite his Hollywood success; he and wife Melanie Griffiths have a luxurious villa in Marbella.

EX-PAT LIFESTYLES

The Costa del Sol has one of the highest concentrations of foreign residents anywhere in Spain. About 1 per cent of the population of this region is not Spanish, and an overwhelming majority of these foreign residents are British. This means that there are English-language newspapers and magazines, several supermarkets selling British essentials like teabags, and all kinds of services, from hairdressers to estate agents, which cater to an English-speaking clientele.

LA RUTA DES PUEBLOS BLANCOS

The Route of the White Villages is a tourist office initiative that highlights some of the loveliest of the white villages in the Sierra de Cádiz, particularly those in and around the Sierra de Grazalema Natural Park. These villages, which include Algodonales, Arcos de la Frontera, Grazalema, Olvera, Ubrique, Villamartín and Zahara de la Sierra, boast traditional houses which are whitewashed to keep out the searing sun.

A Short Stay on the Costa del Sol

DAY 1: MÁLAGA

Morning Start with a typical Spanish breakfast of chocolate *con churros* at the bustling **Café Central** (▷ 36). Then stroll across the old quarter to the foot of the great crag that dominates the city. The vestiges of the **Teatro Romano** (▷ 30) were discovered here and have been substantially rebuilt. Climb through gardens to reach the Moorish fortress, the **Alcazaba** (▷ 25), which boasts spectacular views across the whole coastline, framed by delicate horseshoe arches.

Lunch Back at the bottom of the hill, head for the famous bodega **El Pimpi** (▷ 37) to enjoy a tapas lunch and perhaps a bottle of wine. It's conveniently located around the corner from the Museo Picasso.

Afternoon Spend a couple of hours at the excellent **Museo Picasso** (▷ 26–27). To complete the Picasso experience, wander over to the nearby Plaza de la Merced to see the house in which the celebrated artist was born (**Casa Natal de Picasso**, ▷ 28). This is now a gallery and exhibition space. Stop for a break at one of the numerous cafés and bars that fill the square.

Evening Join the locals and cool off with a stroll along the palm-lined **Paseo del Parque** (▷ 30), a botanic wonderland first laid out in the early 20th century.

Dinner Take a taxi out to the seaside suburb of El Palo to enjoy fabulous Malagueño seafood at **El Tintero** (▷ 38). Return to the old quarter to soak up the lively nightlife. You could perhaps take in a live concert at somewhere like **Onda Pasadena** (▷ 35) or **Trifásico** (▷ 35), or hit one of the glossy nightclubs, such as **Sala Wenge** (▷ 35).

DAY 2: SEVILLA

Morning Take the train from Málaga to **Sevilla** (Seville ▷ 56)—choose from the cheaper regional trains, which take 2 hours 30 mintues, or the more comfortable high-speed train that takes 1 hour 55 minutes. When you arrive at Sevilla's Santa Just station, take a taxi directly to the Gothic cathedral, **La Catedral** and **La Giralda** (▷ 58–59) for magnificent views.

Lunch Tuck into some delicious tapas at the popular **Bar La Giralda** (▷ 74), very close to the cathedral.

Afternoon Visit the breathtaking **Real Alcázar** (▷ 60–61), an enormous royal residence built over the ruins of an Arabic palace that features some of the most exquisite stucco and tile Mudéjar decoration in Spain. Take a break in the jasmine-scented gardens at the back. When you emerge from the palace, abandon your map for a while and plunge into the Barrio Santa Cruz, a whitewashed warren of narrow alleys and flower-filled squares filled with cafés. On the edge of this enchanting neighbourhood is the lovely **Casa de Pilatos** (▷ 57), an aristocratic palace with exquisite gardens.

Evening Stroll down to the river, and cross the Triana bridge to reach the Calle Betis, which flanks the riverside. There are countless bars and restaurants here, most with terraces at the water's edge. It's a great place for a pre-dinner cocktail.

Dinner Make for **La Torrecilla** (▷ 78), a lovely old-fashioned restaurant serving classic local specialties. After dinner head for one of the riverside nightclubs, such as **Capote** (▷ 72), or even take in a summer concert (10pm start) in the gardens of the **Real Alcázar** (▷ tip, 60).

Top 25

TOP
25

► ► ►

ESSENTIAL COSTA DEL SOL TOP 25

Cádiz: Casco Antiguo
▷ 42 A delightful warren of narrow streets with glorious views of Africa.

Córdoba ▷ 43 One of the greatest capitals of Al-Andalus, now a cosmopolitan city.

Córdoba: La Mezquita
▷ 44–45 One of the largest and most extraordinary mosques in Europe.

Zuheros ▷ 92 A lofty white village in a sea of olive groves, this place is perfect for a quiet break.

Tarifa ▷ 62 Laid-back whitewashed town with glorious beaches at the tip of Spain.

Sevilla: Real Alcázar
▷ 60–61 A magical Arabic palace is at the kernel of this royal residence, a fine example of Mudéjar art.

Sevilla: La Catedral and La Giralda ▷ 58–59
The world's largest Gothic cathedral, plus belltower.

Sevilla: Casa de Pilatos
▷ 57 A private mansion with beautiful gardens and exquisitely tiled salons.

Sevilla ▷ 56 Seville is perhaps the most romantic of the great cities of Al-Andalus, with its maze of little lanes.

Ronda ▷ 54–55 This historic town is splayed across a dramatic gorge, spanned by a spectacular bridge.

Puerto Banús ▷ 53
Spot celebrities at the most glamorous and expensive resort on the Costa del Sol.

Parque Natural El Torcal de Antequera ▷ 52
Weird and wonderful stone shapes at this natural park.

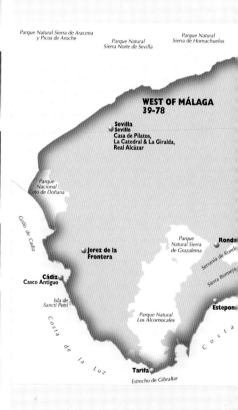

8

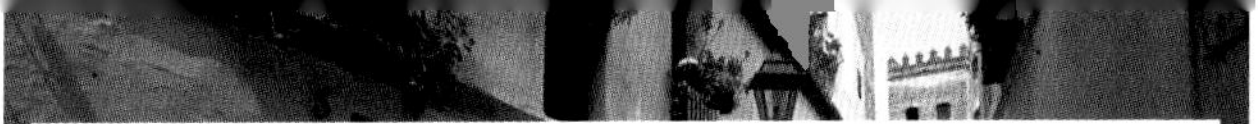

These pages are a quick guide to the Top 25, which are described in more detail later. Here they are listed alphabetically, and the tinted background shows which area they are in.

ESSENTIAL COSTA DEL SOL TOP 25

Map labels:

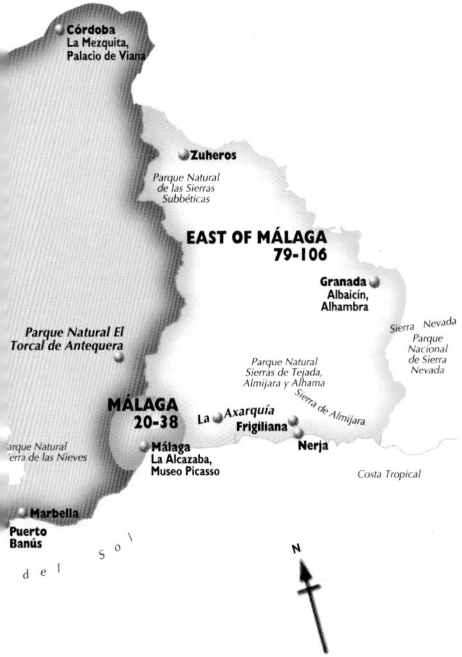

Córdoba
La Mezquita,
Palacio de Viana

Zuheros

Parque Natural
de las Sierras
Subbéticas

EAST OF MÁLAGA
79–106

Parque Natural El
Torcal de Antequera

Granada
Albaicín,
Alhambra

Sierra Nevada
Parque
Nacional
de Sierra
Nevada

Parque Natural
Sierras de Tejada,
Almijara y Alhama

Sierra de Almijara

MÁLAGA
20–38

La Axarquía
Frigiliana

Parque Natural
erra de las Nieves

Málaga
La Alcazaba,
Museo Picasso

Nerja

Costa Tropical

Marbella

Puerto
Banús

d e l   S o l

N

◀ ◀ ◀

Shopping

The Costa del Sol is an excellent destination for shopping. Whether you are looking for designer fashions, handmade local crafts, tasty local cheeses and hams, a few bottles of the regional wines and sherries, or just a bottle of fragrant olive oil, there's something to suit all tastes and pockets. While the big cities, particularly Málaga, Sevilla, Córdoba and Granada, have the widest range of shops, the cosmopolitan resorts are all very well geared toward shoppers.

Crafts and Souvenirs

Many of the crafts popular in Andalucía have a long history dating back to Arabic times. There are beautiful ceramics, many of which still bear ancient designs that recall the era of Al-Andalus. Woodwork and marquetry is also popular, particularly in Granada. Leatherwork has long been a local craft, and Ubrique (▷ 67) is one of many villages that are still dedicated to the production of leather goods. Traditional shawls (*mantillas*), haircombs and flamenco dresses can be found throughout Andalucía, but the best selection can be found in Sevilla.

Local Goodies

Many of the smaller villages specialize in local cheeses, hams and charcuterie, which can usually be vacuum-packed (*al vacío* in Spanish) to be brought home. Olive oil is widely available, but some of the finest comes from the Sierra de Cádiz (particularly around Olvera). The Jerez

---

OPENING HOURS

In the cities and inland towns, shops are usually open from around 9.30 or 10 in the morning until 1.30 or 2, and then again from 4 or 4.30 until 8 or 9. They often close on Saturday afternoons and all day Sunday. Larger shops and department stores stay open all day, and often close at 9 or 10pm. However, along the coast, shops that are geared toward tourists regularly open daily in high season.

An array of souvenirs—from olive oil to guitars and ceramic bowls to leather handbags—on sale on the Costa del Sol

region is, of course, synonymous with sherry, and all the bodegas offer their own products for sale. You could also pick up local wines from Ronda, or the delicious sweet wine *jarel*, which comes from La Axarquía. The hams from Jabugo (northwest of Sevilla) and Trevélez (southeast of Granada) are considered among the finest in Spain.

Where to Buy

For international designer fashions, head for Puerto Banús, where you'll find every major brand from Gucci to Chanel. All the cities have several branches of the most popular Spanish fashion chains, including Zara, Mango and Camper. For one-stop shopping, the Spanish department store, El Corte Inglés, can provide everything from plug-adaptors to gourmet groceries. Tourist offices are an excellent source of information, with listings of local artisans.

Markets

Almost every town and village has a market. In the big cities, such as Málaga, there are large covered municipal markets, which are always buzzing with life. In smaller places, the market tends to be an outdoor affair that takes place one day a week (tourist offices can give you a list of local markets). In all markets, you'll find fabulously fresh local produce—the perfect makings for a picnic. Along the coast, particularly in high season, you'll find numerous craft markets, which often feature North African crafts, flip-flops and swimming costumes, as well as some local souvenirs.

SALES

Bargain hunters shouldn't miss the sales in Spain, when prices are slashed considerably. The summer sales begin on the 1 July and the winter sales begin on 7 January. Sales usually last for about a month, but you'll often find bargain rails in shops for another month or so. The Zara sale is famously good, and in some places shoppers begin queuing long before the doors open.

Outdoor Activities

There are now more than 60 golf courses on the Costa del Sol, or 'Costa del Golf'. Sailing and watersports are very popular, and the region counts some of the finest marinas in Spain. In the inland regions, hiking, horse-riding and bird-watching are favourite activities, but adventure sports are becoming increasingly popular.

Golf

Golf has become one of the biggest draws of the Costa del Sol, thanks to the combination of fabulous weather and magnificent courses. The Costa del Sol tourism organization publishes a very useful booklet listing all the courses and their facilities.

Sailing and Watersports

There are numerous marinas along the Costa del Sol, including the Benalmádena marina, which is considered one of the finest in the world. Most marinas host sailing schools, with a wide range of courses for people of all ages and abilities. For those who enjoy surfing, kitesurfing and windsurfing, head for Tarifa and the Costa de la Luz. Visit the website www.visitacostadelsol.com.

Hiking, Horse-riding and Adventure

The mountainous interior of Andalucía is a paradise for walkers, bird-watchers and those interested in horse-riding or adventure activities such as mountain biking, pot-holing and mountaineering. Tourist offices can provide information on local tour operators.

SKIING IN ANDALUCÍA

Andalucia is one of the only places in the world where you can go skiing in the morning and head for the beach in the afternoon. The lofty peaks of the Sierra Nevada near Granada boast Europe's most southerly ski-station, which is usually open from December to April. Comprehensive information on the ski station and its facilities is available at www.cetursa.es.

From top: Kitesurfing; anyone for golf?; horse-riding along the beach; windsurfing on the Costa del Sol

Costa del Sol by Night

The Costa del Sol provides every imaginable form of entertainment, from classical music concerts in sublime settings such as the Alhambra, to glossy nightclubs where you'll have to dress to impress. Every resort offers numerous pubs, bars and clubs to suit all tastes, and the major cities all boast fine theatres. Best of all are the village festivals, with traditional music, parades and carousing on the streets.

Annual Festivals and Events
Some of the biggest festivals on the Andalucian calendar include the *Semana Santa* (Holy Week), celebrated throughout Spain but with special fervour in Sevilla. It's followed soon after by the hedonistic *Feria de Abríl*, when everyone dresses up in their finest flamenco outfits for several days of fun. Carnival is a wild and colourful event, particularly in Cádiz. Performing arts events include the celebrated Córdoba guitar festival (held in July) and Granada's international festival of music and dance (end June–early July). Book accommodation early during these periods. For more information on festivals, ▷ 114.

Nightclubs
The Costa del Sol is packed with mega-clubs —huge nightclubs, which usually have outdoor dance spaces. Outdoor bars, which are often open only during the summer, are called *terrazas*. The most exclusive clubs are clustered around Marbella and Puerto Banús.

From top: Enjoying a night out; a view of Málaga at night; Sevilla restaurant; La Giralda, Sevilla

FLAMENCO

Nothing captures the spirit of Andalucía quite like flamenco. Jerez is considered the cradle of the art, but it's popular throughout the region. There are numerous *tablaos*, flamenco shows that may include dinner, which are geared toward tourists. These are always fun, but they lack the spirit of spontaneity at the heart of flamenco. If you are lucky, you may come across an impromptu performance in one of the bars of Granada or Sevilla.

Eating Out

Andalucian cuisine is based on fresh, local ingredients—fresh seafood from the Mediterranean and Atlantic, succulent beef from the glossy black cattle that you'll see throughout the region, game and superb hams from the mountains, and plump tomatoes and vegetables from the plains.

Local Specialties

The classic favourite along the coast is *pescaíto frito*—a platter of small fish tossed in batter and fried in olive oil, which is also called *pescadito frito* or *frito Malagueña*. The refreshing cold soups, *gazpacho* and *salmorejo* (a thicker version of *gazpacho*) are wonderful in summer. *Rabo de toro* (ox tail) is a classic, slowly simmered with vegetables and herbs until tender. Try the famous sherries from Jerez, as well as delicious local wines from the Ronda region and elsewhere.

Where to Eat

Tapas are central to Andalucian cuisine, and these delicious small snacks are served in numerous tapas bars throughout the region. Many tapas bars have adjoining *comedors* (dining rooms) for more substantial fare. *Tavernas* and *mesones* are generally traditional inns, and *restaurantes* run the gamut from small family businesses to sleek designer eateries. *Marisquerías* are establishments that specialize in shellfish.

EATING ON A BUDGET

Many restaurants serve a fixed-price lunch menu (*menú del día*) on weekdays—this is the best way to dine at the finest restaurants for a bargain price. These are less common in the busy resorts, but all the major towns and cities have plenty of restaurants that offer this great deal. Almost every town boasts at least one market, where you can pick up wonderful local produce—tomatoes, hams—to make a fabulous picnic, surely one of the most pleasant ways to eat a meal.

The choice of restaurants and the variety of cuisine is a highlight of a visit to the Costa del Sol

Restaurants by Cuisine

The restaurants on this page are listed by cuisine. For detailed descriptions, see the individual listings in Costa del Sol by Area.

ANDALUCIAN

El Angelote (▷ 74)
La Bodeguilla (▷ 103)
El Caballo Rojo (▷ 74)
Cádiz el Chico (▷ 74)
La Carbona (▷ 74)
Casa Luque (▷ 103)
Casa Pablo (▷ 75)
El Chinitas (▷ 36)
El Choto (▷ 75)
El Churrasco (▷ 75)
El Gallo (▷ 77)
Garden Restaurant (▷ 105)
El Huerto de Juan Ranas (▷ 105)
Mariano (▷ 37)
Merchán 1955 (▷ 77)
Mesón Juderia (▷ 77)
Mesón los Palancos (▷ 105)
Mesón Riofrío (▷ 106)
El Palacete (▷ 37)
Pedro Romero (▷ 77)
Portofino (▷ 78)
Restaurante San Fernando (▷ 78)
Salmorejo (▷ 38)
Sevilla (▷ 106)
Taberna San Miguel (▷ 78)
La Torrecilla (▷ 78)
Venta de Alfarnate (▷ 106)

ASIAN/FUSION

Asako (▷ 36)
Citron (▷ 36)
Hotel la Tartana (▷ 105)
Lansang (▷ 105)
Mirador de Cerro Gordo (▷ 106)
Palacio Wok (▷ 37)
Scarletta's (▷ 106)

CAFÉS

Bar Juanito (▷ 74)
Café Central (▷ 36)
Comoloco (▷ 36)
Creperie Santa Fé (▷ 75)
Erwaya (▷ 36)
Freiduria las Flores (▷ 77)
Heladería Tiggiani (▷ 105)
Lechuga (▷ 37)

CONTEMPORARY

El Choco (▷ 75)
Tragabuches (▷ 78)

MEDITERRANEAN

Arroceria la Pepa (▷ 74)
Clandestino (▷ 36)
Il Laboratorio (▷ 37)
El Pipeo (▷ 37)
Picasso (▷ 77)
Pizzeria Diego (▷ 78)
Pizzeria Trastevere (▷ 38)
Retruque (▷ 38)
Sosúa (▷ 38)

NORTH AFRICAN

La Mandragora (▷ 77)
Souk (▷ 78)
El Tragaluz (▷ 106)

SEAFOOD

Casa Juan (▷ 75)
Cunini (▷ 105)
Miguelito el Cariñoso (▷ 37)
El Peñon (▷ 106)
El Tintero (▷ 38)

SOUTH AMERICAN

El Dorado (▷ 75)
Tango (▷ 78)
Vino Mio (▷ 38)

TAPAS BARS

Antigua Casa de Guardia (▷ 36)
Bar Brenes (▷ 74)
Bar la Giralda (▷ 74)
Bar Restaurante Pesetas (▷ 103)
Los Barriles (▷ 103)
Bodega Francisco (▷ 103)
Bodega Sabor Andaluz (▷ 74)
Bodega Saint Germain (▷ 103)
Casa Julio (▷ 103)
La Cepa (▷ 103)
Cerveceria el Tonelito (▷ 75)
Chikito (▷ 105)
De Costa a Costa (▷ 105)
El Gallo Azul (▷ 77)
Los Melli (▷ 77)
Museo del Vino (▷ 106)
El Pimpi (▷ 37)
Taberna el Trasiego (▷ 38)

VEGETARIAN

Cañadu (▷ 36)
El Vegetariano de la Alcazabilla (▷ 38)

If you Like...

However you'd like to spend your time on the Costa del Sol, these ideas should help you tailor your perfect visit. Each suggestion has a fuller write-up elsewhere in the book.

TRADITIONAL CRAFTS

Buy beautiful handmade gifts at Versión Original, Málaga (▷ 33), including ceramics and jewellery.
Get the best quality handmade guitars at Guitarreria Germán Pérez Barranco, Granada (▷ 99–100).
For the best in local ceramics try Grenada's Cerámica Fabre (▷ 99), in alluring hues of blue and green.

TASTY TAPAS

Sample the giddying range of tapas at Bar La Giralda (▷ 74), in the heart of Sevilla.
You'll discover award-winning gourmet tapas at El Gallo Azul, Jerez (▷ 77).
Try the celebrated local classic El Pimpi, Málaga (▷ 37), with fabulous tapas.

Pretty ceramics for sale (top); tasty tapas (above)

KEEPING TO A TIGHT BUDGET

Go to a free festival such as the wonderful ones of La Axarquía (▷ 89).
Picnic in the hills in the numerous wonderful natural parks, such as Parque Natural El Torcal de Antequera (▷ 52).
Lose yourself in sun, sea and sand: the Costa del Sol's famous beaches, such as Nerja (▷ 90), are all free.

Benalmádena beach (above); a seafood platter (below)

FRESH SEAFOOD

Eat at an old favourite—El Tintero, Málaga (▷ 38)—a cheerful, traditional seaside eaterie, which hasn't changed in decades.
Feast on fried fish to go at Freiduria Las Flores, Cádiz (▷ 75), a celebrated local institution.
Magnificently set on the rocks, El Peñon, Salobreña (▷ 106), has sublime seafood.

FLAMENCO RHYTHMS

La Taberna Flamenca (▷ 73) in Jerez, where flamenco was born, is the place for dinner and a flamenco show.
Learn about flamenco at the Flamenco Museum, the Cueva Maria la Canastera, Granada (▷ 101).
Visit the only authentic *peña* (flamenco folk club) on the Costa Tropical—the Taberna Flamenca Ricardo De La Juana, Almuñécar (▷ 102).

Flamenco dancer (above); Parque Natural El Torcal de Antequera (below)

THE GREAT OUTDOORS

Discover surreal limestone rock formations in a lunar landscape at the Parque Natural El Torcal de Antequera (▷ 52).
Visit one of the greatest wetland reserves in Europe at Parque Nacional Coto de Doñana (▷ 67).
Take to the glorious hills dotted with rural villages and terraced orchards in the La Axarquía region (▷ 88–89) and explore by car or on foot.

MEMORIES OF AL-ANDALUS

One of the greatest mosques of the Islamic world is La Mezquita, Córdoba, (▷ 44–45).
Visit a glittering Mudéjar palace, the Real Alcázar, Sevilla (▷ 60–61).
Surely the greatest monument to Al-Andalus is the Alhambra, Granada, (▷ 86–87), a magical palace.

Real Alcázar, Sevilla (above); Frigiliana (below)

AUTHENTIC VILLAGES

Frigiliana is possibly the prettiest village on the Costa del Sol (▷ 82).
A lovely white gem, Zuheros (▷ 92) surrounded by olive groves, should not be missed.
Cómpeta (▷ 93) is surely the prettiest village in the rugged Axarquía hills.

KEEPING THE KIDS HAPPY

Check out the parrots and tropical plants at the popular Ornithological Park, Almuñécar (▷ 93).

Go all aboard for whale and dolphin-watching from Gibraltar (▷ 66) or Tarifa (▷ 62).

Take to the waves on a surfboard, skipper a windsurfer or paddle a kayak with Windsurf La Herradura (▷ 102).

PARTYING 'TILL DAWN

Try the sleek and stylish club Casanova Lounge Club, Málaga (▷ 34).

Dance at the breezy, riverside outdoor club Capote, Seville (▷ 72).

Experience a classic on the Costa del Sol—the massive nightclub, Fun Beach, Torremolinos (▷ 72).

Improbably set in a shopping centre try the club Mae West, Granada (▷ 101).

STYLISH HIDEAWAYS

Stay at a chic little inn in an enchanting village and book a table at La Botica, Véjer de la Frontera (▷ 109).

The Beach House, Mijas Costa (▷ 110) has a stunning seafront location and minimalist design.

For true romance stay at the villa with views of the Alhambra at Carmen de Cobertizo, Granada (▷ 110).

The most elegant, aristocratic guesthouse in Sevilla's old quarter is Casa No.7 (▷ 112).

Trying out a kayak (top); there is plenty of choice if you want to party (above)

LOCAL WINES

Still the best place to try *Málaga Dulce* is Antigua Casa de Guardia, Málaga (▷ 36), founded in 1840.

Take a tipple at a sherry tasting in the bodegas of Jerez (▷ 48–49).

Head for Cómpeta's wine festival in August (▷ 93), when the fountains run with sweet local wine.

Wines to sample or to take home

Costa del Sol by Area

MÁLAGA

WEST OF MÁLAGA

EAST OF MÁLAGA

Málaga

Authentic and welcoming, the handsome provincial capital of Málaga has plenty to offer besides the standard Costa delights of sun, sea and sand. There's a clutch of excellent museums, a vibrant old quarter and a pair of Moorish castles dizzily set high on a clifftop overlooking the sea.

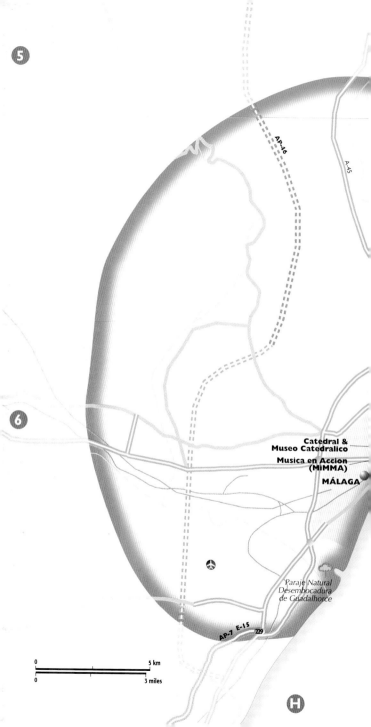

5

6

AP-46

A-45

Catedral &
Museo Catedralico

Musica en Accion
(MiMMA)

MÁLAGA

Paraje Natural
Desembocadura
de Guadalhorce

AP-7 E-15   229

0 ——————— 5 km

0 ——————— 3 miles

H

Parque
Natural Montes
de Málaga

Ecomuseo
Lagar de
Torrijos

A-7

Málaga

Iglesia de Casa Natal
Santiago   de Picasso

Museo   Teatro Romano
Picasso   Castillo de Gibralfaro
          La Alcazaba
          La Malagueta
          Playa de la Malagueta

Paseo del
Parque

Centro de Arte
Contemporáneo
de Málaga

Ensenada
de Málaga

Costa   del   Sol

N

J

Málaga

Málaga fountain (left); courtyard in the Museo des Artes (middle); the Town Hall (right)

THE BASICS

www.malagaturismo.com

H6

Plaza Marina 11, tel 952 12 20 20; Apr–end Oct Mon–Fri 9–7, Sat–Sun 10–7; Nov–end Mar Mon–Fri 9–6, Sat–Sun 10–6

HIGHLIGHTS

- Museo Picasso
- Picasso's former home
- Old quarter
- Alcazaba
- Beachfront restaurants
- Shopping opportunities

Málaga, still mystifyingly overlooked by many holiday-makers, is the most enchanting Spanish city on the Costa del Sol. The Museo Picasso has raised Málaga's profile—but you'll still find more Spanish than tourists on its streets.

Picasso's city Málaga is proud of its connection with Pablo Picasso, perhaps the most famous 20th-century artist, who was born here in 1881. In 2003, the city inaugurated the Museo Picasso (▷ 26–27), which boasts a superb collection of Picasso's work and is set in an attractive 16th-century palace. Committed fans of the artist can also visit his former home, the Casa Natal de Picasso (▷ 28).

The old quarter The majestic baroque cathedral is at the heart of Málaga's atmospheric old quarter. Explore the winding alleys with their shops and tranquil cafés, delightful squares and churches. Perched on a hilltop overlooking the old quarter and dramatically dominating the whole city is the Moorish castle, La Alcazaba (▷ 25), which boasts spectacular views.

Further afield The city's contemporary art museum, the Centro de Arte Contemporáneo de Málaga (▷ 29), hosts superb temporary exhibitions. This area is also where you'll find the most convenient shopping. Join in the evening stroll, the *paseo*, when Malagueños parade along the leafy Paseo del Parque, before heading to the beachfront restaurants in La Malagueta and El Palo.

Málaga: La Alcazaba

View of the Alcazaba and castle (left); inside the Alcazaba (right)

The city of Málaga is dominated by the romantic ruins of the Alcazaba, the best-preserved Arabic fortress in Spain. Set in palm-studded gardens on a lofty cliff-top, it offers a glorious, bird's-eye view over the city and out to sea.

The gardens The approach to the fortress complex begins at the foot of the hill, near the Teatro Romano (▷ 30), and meanders steeply upward via a series of zig-zag paths, shaded by palm trees. Away from the hubbub of the city below you glimpse into the world of the Nasrids who constructed the complex over the ruins of a Roman fortress in the 8th century. Of the original three rings of defensive walls, two sets survive, studded with gateways with traces of intricate decoration.

Fortress complex Once through the gates, you arrive at the main fortress complex on the crest of the hill. A strategic site, it has been occupied since Roman times, but most of what survives today was built in the 11th century by King Badis of Granada, who dramatically expanded an 8th-century kernel. The complex contained three palaces, a residential area and a watchtower (the Torre del Homenaje). The delicate horseshoe-shaped arches have fabulous sea views.

Archaeological museum A section of the first Nasrid palace has been restored to house the city's Museo Arquelógico, which contains finds from the first Phoenician settlements, along with Roman lamps and amphorae, and Arabic ceramics.

THE BASICS

➕ d2
✉ Calle Alcazabilla 2
☎ No phone
🕐 Nov–end Mar Tue–Sun 8.30–7; Apr–end Oct Tue–Sun 9.30–8 (museum opening times the same)
🍽 Several near the entrance, plus a summer kiosk within the complex
♿ Few
💲 Inexpensive

HIGHLIGHTS

● Views over the Mediterranean
● Horseshoe arches
● Torre del Homenaje
● Archaeological Museum
● Stroll along the ramparts
● Torre del Cristo

TIP

● Get the combined admission ticket with the Castillo Gibralfaro, which includes transport on a shuttle bus, and avoid the dusty walk up to the second castle.

Málaga:
Museo Picasso

- Representations of all Picasso's artistic periods
- *Portrait of Paul in a White Cap* (1923)
- *Músico Sentado* (1950)
- *Three Doves* (1960)
- Phoenician walls

TIP

- Aficionados of Picasso's work should visit the city in October, when Málaga celebrates the artist with exhibitions, talks and all kinds of special events.

Housed in a beautifully restored 16th-century palace, the Museo Picasso boasts a relatively small, but choice, collection of works. Unlike other museums dedicated to the artist, they span all periods of the artist's career—making Málaga's collection unique.

History of the museum The kernel of the collection was donated by Picasso's daughter-in-law and grandson to ensure that the city in which Picasso was born should hold a significant collection.

The collection The displays start with the earliest realist works created by a child prodigy, continue through the famous paintings of the Blue and Rose periods, and include many celebrated Cubist and Surrealist works, which broke with all conventions.

The attractive internal courtyard of the Museo Picasso (left); spacious, light and airy galleries display Picasso's work to great effect (right)

Because many of the works on display have been donated or loaned by family members, there is an appealing intimacy to the collection, which includes a number of portraits. Perhaps most famous of these is the *Retrato de Paulo con Gorro Blanco* (*Portrait of Paul in a White Cap*, 1923), with the painter's son gazing out with a child's direct and unsettling expression. Among the ceramics, look out for the quirky black-and-white owl and the seated musican (*Músico Sentado*, 1950).

The palace The 16th-century Palacio de Buenavista was built for Diego de Cazalla, who took the city from the Arabs in the 1480s, and is typically Andalucian in its melding of Renaissance and Mudéjar decorative elements. Sections of a wall built by the Phoencians have been sensitively displayed in the lower level of the museum.

THE BASICS

www.museopicassomalaga. org
🟦 d2
✉ Calle San Agustín 8
☎ 902 44 33 77
🕐 Sun–Thu 10–8, Fri–Sat 10–9
🍴 Café
♿ Good
💰 Moderate
❓ Free admission last Sun of the month up to 3pm

More to See

CASA NATAL DE PICASSO
www.fundacionpicasso.es
The house in which Pablo Picasso was born on 25 October 1881 is now a museum, documentation centre for specialists and gallery space. Temporary exhibitions, usually by contemporary artists, are held on the ground floor. On the first floor, the Pablo Ruiz Picasso Foundation Museum contains a small but wonderful collection of the artist's bold ceramics, a collection of engravings and some exquisitely illustrated books.
➕ d1 (fold-out map) ✉ Plaza Merced 15
☎ 952 06 02 15 ⏰ Daily 9.30–8 💶 Free to gallery; inexpensive to museum

CASTILLO DE GIBRALFARO
This hill was first occupied by a Phoenican watchtower. The Gibralfaro castle was built by Yusuf I of Granada, and was subsequently occupied by Fernando V after the Reconquest of Málaga in the late 15th century. An interpretation centre provides an insight into the castle's original function and the grounds offer magnificent views over the sea and as far as the Straits of Gibraltar on clear days.
➕ e2 ✉ Camino Gibralfaro 11 ☎ 952 12 20 20 ⏰ Nov–end Mar daily 9–6; Apr–end Oct 9–8 💶 Inexpensive

CATEDRAL AND MUSEO CATEDRALICO
Málaga's enormous cathedral, like so many in Spain, was built over the remnants of a mosque. Begun in the 16th century, but not completed for another two centuries, the interior is largely Gothic and Renaissance, while the splendid pink-and-white-marble façade is classic baroque. The unfinished belltower has given the cathedral its affectionate nickname, 'La Manquita', or 'One-Armed Lady'. The notable 17th-century choir stalls of mahogany and cedarwood were designed by Luis Ortiz. The Cathedral Museum contains a dusty collection of antique silver plate, religious paintings and vestments.
➕ c2 ✉ Calle Molina Lario 9
☎ 952 21 59 17 ⏰ Mon–Fri 10–6, Sat 10–5
💶 Free to cathedral; inexpensive to museum

The Moorish castle stands guard over Málaga town

Málaga's impressive cathedral tower

CENTRO DE ARTE CONTEMPORÁNEO DE MÁLAGA

www.cacmalaga.org

Málaga's Contemporary Art Centre (CAC) occupies a sleek, white Rationalist building erected in the 1920s. The CAC Málaga opened as a result of the demand from local people whose cultural interests have been growing. It has become one of the most exciting cultural institutions in Andalucía since it opened in 2003. It hosts excellent temporary exhibitions by outstanding Spanish and international contemporary artists, including Louise Bourgeois, the Chapman brothers and Rodney Graham, as well as offering a varied programme of cultural events.

➕ a3 ✉ Calle Alemania 2 ☎ 952 12 00 55 ⏱ Mid-Jun to mid-Sep Tue–Sun 10–2, 5–9; mid-Sep to mid-Jun Tue–Sun 10–8 ♿ Good 💷 Free

ECOMUSEU LAGAR DE TORRIJOS

Just 5km (3 miles) north of Málaga's city centre is the Parque Natural Montes de Málaga, a verdant expanse of forested hills crisscrossed with hiking paths. In the little village of Torrijos, an engaging eco-museum has been carefully restored to show how life was lived in these hills a century or so ago.

➕ H6 ✉ Carretera del Colmenar s/n, Torrijos ☎ 951 04 21 00 ⏱ Thu–Fri 10–2 (closed Thu in summer), Sat–Sun and public hols 10–4

IGLESIA DE SANTIAGO

This is the oldest church in Málaga, founded by Isabella and Ferdinand (who were jointly known as the Catholic Kings) in 1490. It boasts some of the finest decorative Mudéjar brickwork in the city, carried out by Arab craftsmen who remained after the city's reconquest. The tower is particularly ornate, with delicate patterns exquisitely wrought in brick. It was here that Picasso was baptized in 1881.

➕ d2 ✉ Calle Granada 78 ☎ 952 21 96 61 ⏱ Tue–Sat 9–1.30, 6–8 (no visits during services) 💷 Free

The exterior of the Centro de Arte Contemporáneo de Málaga

Olive trees are abundant around Málaga

LA MALAGUETA AND THE BEACHES

Just beyond the city's bullring is the former fishermen's neighbourhood of La Malagueta. This is where Málaga's beaches begin. The nearby beachfront suburbs of El Palo and Pedregalejo are famous for their seafood restaurants.

➕ d4–e4 (fold-out map)

MUSEU INTERACTIVO DE LA MÚSICA (MIMMA)

www.musicaenaccion.com

This is perhaps the most entertaining museum in the city: dedicated to music, it offers an interactive experience that will thrill adults and children alike. Visitors can hear curious and rare instruments, make their own music, and even see how some of the very first instruments, made from human skulls, were played. Check the website for details of concert cycles.

➕ c2 ✉ Plaza de la Marina 3 ☎ 952 21 04 40 🕐 Mon–Fri 10–2, 6–8, Sat–Sun 11–3, 4.30–8.30 ♿ Good 🎫 Inexpensive

PASEO DEL PARQUE

Filled with fountains and pools, this botanic wonderland was first laid out between 1912 and 1919 but has recently been handsomely restored. Specimens of plants and trees have been brought here from all over the world. The palm-lined avenue is a favourite for the evening *paseo*.

➕ c2–d3 ✉ Paseo del Parque ☎ No phone 🕐 Always open ♿ Good 🎫 Free

TEATRE ROMANO

Malaga's Roman theatre was built during the 1st century AD, but was abandoned sometime during the 3rd century. The Arabs plundered the stone to build the Alcazaba fortress, which looms above it on the clifftop, and the remnants were gradually buried over the centuries. It emerged once again in 1951, and has been considerably restored.

➕ d2 ✉ Calle Alcazabilla 9 ☎ 951 04 14 00 🕐 Apr–end Oct Tue–Sat 10–9, Sun 10–2.30; Nov–end Mar Tue–Sat 9–7, Sun 10–2.30 ♿ Few ❓ Guided tour available

La Malagueta beach

Statue in the Paseo del Parque, Málaga

A Walk Around Málaga

This walk explores Málaga's old centre, passing the cathedral and the Roman theatre, and some of the sites associated with Picasso.

DISTANCE: 2km (1.2 miles)   **ALLOW:** 2 hours

START   **END**

PLAZA DE LA MARINA   **PASEO DEL PARQUE**
✚ c2   ✚ c3–d3

① Start at the Tourist Office at Plaza de la Marina, cross the street and head up Calle Marqués de Larios—the city's main shopping street, and a good place to pick up souvenirs.

⑧ The road heads toward the Plaza de la Marina, your starting point. Just before you reach the square, you'll see the Paseo del Parque on your left.

② Turn right onto Calle Salinas. On reaching Plaza del Obispo, gaze at the lavish baroque bishop's palace and have a drink at one of the bar terraces. Go left onto Calle Molina Lario.

⑦ You will see the 1st-century AD Teatro Romano (▷ 30) on the left. Continue down Calle Alcazabilla until you reach the splendid former Customs House, now being converted into the Museo de Málaga. The road becomes Calle de la Cortina de la Muelle.

③ The cathedral (▷ 28) is on your right. Bear left onto Calle Santa Maria; passing the Iglesia del Sagrario behind the cathedral.

⑥ Picasso was born at No.15, now a museum and gallery. Cross the square, and the adjoining Plaza María Guerrero, to join teeming Calle Alcazabilla with its enticing terrace cafés and bars.

④ Turn left onto pedestrianized Calle San Agustín, to the Museo Picasso (▷ 26–27). Next continue along Calle San Agustin to reach the 15th-century Iglesia de Santiago.

⑤ Here Picasso was baptized. Beyond it is the Plaza de la Merced.

Shopping

ADICTO URBAN SHOP

Street fashion for young men and women can be found at this hip boutique, which also stocks a select range of shoes, bags and accessories. The range of T-shirts is particularly good. You can also pick up fliers for clubs, concerts and special events.
🞣 c1 (fold-out map) 🖂 Calle Carretería 94 ☎ 952 21 38 97

ALFAJAR

www.alfajar.net
The beautiful range of colourful Andalucian ceramics for sale here have been inspired by original Roman, Phoenician and Iberian designs. Choose from jugs, bowls, tiles, vases, platters and much more.
🞣 c2 🖂 Calle Císter 13 ☎ 952 21 12 72

ARTE POSTRE

www.artepostre.es
The name says it all: 'the art of dessert'. Chocoholics and anyone with a sweet tooth should make a beeline to this temple to the best things in life: cakes, tarts, pastries, chocolates and bon bons, all works of art and beautifully packaged.
🞣 c2 🖂 Calle Cerezuela s/n ☎ 952 64 18 98

CACAO SAMPAKA

www.cacaosampaka.com
This is part of a small Barcelona-based chain of chocolatiers, and is paradise for all chocoholics. Sleek, contemporary packaging and original recipes (among them white chocolate with cinnamon) make for wonderful gifts. Don't miss the divine hot chocolate mix.
🞣 c2 🖂 Calle Granada 49 ☎ 952 22 33 10

CACHE

Part of a reliable local chain, this store sells leather shoes for men and women at very reasonable prices. There is also a small selection of co-ordinating bags and belts.
🞣 a1 (fold-out map) 🖂 Calle Armengual de la Mota 30 ☎ 952 30 77 74

CARAMELO

www.caramelo.com
Located on the city's main shopping street, Caramelo offers top-quality clothes for men, including elegant suits, casual wear and accessories. Prices are surprisingly moderate, and good value for the quality.
🞣 c2 🖂 Calle Marqués de Larios 2 ☎ 952 22 86 84

EL CORTE INGLÉS

www.elcorteingles.es
An outpost of the giant Spanish department store, which sells just about everything: make-up, perfumes, fashion, electrical goods, books, objects for the home and much more. There's an excellent supermarket, with a wide range of top-quality produce, and a café. It's the best place in the city for one-stop shopping.
🞣 a2 🖂 Avenida de Andalucía 4-6 ☎ 952 07 65 00

ATARAZANAS MARKET

Málaga's central market on Calle Atarazanas is a sensory wonderland: stalls piled high with a myriad of fruit and vegetables, steel slabs with glistening fish, pungent displays of cured meats and local cheeses. The building, a 19th-century construction, incorporates an exquisite 15th-century Arabic horseshoe arch. Note that most stalls close at 2pm and on Sunday. The surrounding bars and cafés are good spots for an inexpensive lunch in between sightseeing.

EVALO REGALOS

Fun gifts to satisfy kids of all ages. This shop has all kinds of amusing items, from T-shirts and mugs to posters and teddy bears. There's also a selection of jewellery and small decorative objects for the home. Logos range from Batman to Betty Boop.
🞣 d2 🖂 Calle Granada 67 ☎ 952 22 81 46

FLAMENKA

www.flamenka.com
Passionately dedicated to the world of flamenco, the owners of this shop have made this a sure stop for all fans. Come

here for books, CDs, musical instruments and all the latest news on flamenco events taking place in the area.

🔶 b1 (fold-out map)
✉ Pasillo de Santa Isabel 5
☎ 952 21 47 78

GALERIAS GOYA

This small shopping centre is conveniently located in the heart of the city with shops selling everything from shoes to fashion (try Stroop for fabulous T-shirts) and even a curious little place with everything you need for a fancy dress party.

🔶 c1 (fold-out map)
✉ Plaza Uncibay 3 ☎ 952 22 56 50

HOSS INTROPIA

This is an outpost of an excellent Basque designer, with gorgeous and original fashions and accessories for women. Designs are strikingly unique, often in luxurious fabrics such as silk, often using colourful prints. Prices are moderate, particularly considering the high quality. The shoes and bags are equally original and highly desirable.

🔶 c1 (fold-out map)
✉ Plaza de la Constitución 6
☎ 952 06 23 76

MAPAS Y COMPAÑIA

www.mapasycia.com
This excellent shop sells a wide range of guidebooks and maps in several languages. They also stock travel literature, novels,

greeting cards, globes, compasses and posters. Staff are well informed and very helpful. The wood panelled shop, with its leafy palms, is a delightful place to browse.

🔶 b1 (fold-out map)
✉ C/Compañia 33 (at the intersection with Fajardo)
☎ 952 60 88 15

MASSIMO DUTTI

www.massimodutti.com
This popular Spanish chain offers good quality Italian-designed clothing for men, women and children at a reasonable price. Formal wear, business attire and casual wear are all available.

🔶 c2 ✉ Calle Marqués de Larios 4 ☎ 952 21 69 34

SUPERSKUNK

www.superskunk.es
Brightly coloured, fun,

UNSTOPPABLE CHAINS

In recent years, Spain has produced some of the world's most successful fashion chains. Foremost among them is Zara, which offers style on a budget for men and women and children as well as a new line in interior furnishings and decorative objects. Also popular are Mango, which has just introduced a new men's line, and Camper, for comfortable, but fashionable shoes. You'll find numerous chain stores along the Calle Marqués de Larios.

often retro-style, designer gifts and objects for the home can be found in this colourful shop. You'll find a wide range of items from furnishings, to beach chairs, to a select array of clothes and accessories.

🔶 d2 ✉ Calle Granada 52
☎ 952 65 78 00

VERSIÓN ORIGINAL

This small, original and charming shop sells jewellery, ceramics and engravings made by top artisans.

🔶 d2 ✉ Calle Granada 71
☎ 952 60 97 37

VINO CALIDAD

www.vinocalidad.com
In a small street, this wine shop and club provides good advice from real experts on Spanish wine. There is an enormous range of wines available, including selections from the best national bodegas. Join one of their wine tasting courses.

🔶 d2 ✉ Calle Hilera 4
☎ 952 61 75 60

ZARA

www.zara.com
Probably the world's most famous Spanish fashion brand, Zara offers contemporary style on a budget. This is just one of several branches around the city, and has departments for men, women and children.

🔶 b2 ✉ Calle Liborio García 10 ☎ 952 22 24 06

Entertainment and Activities

BEBOP BLUES & JAZZ CLUB

A big favourite with jazz fans, the Bebop is legendary in the Málaga region. It's located near the beaches in the Malagueta neighbourhood. There's a great atmosphere, some excellent live jazz and blues, and, perhaps best of all, concerts are usually free. Although the bar is open daily, gigs take place on Thursday, Friday and Saturday nights at 11pm; doors open at 10.30pm.

➕ e3 ✉ Calle Arenal 1 ☎ 607 92 30 08

CAFÉ CALLE DE BRUSELAS

www.calledebruselas.com
A classic on Málaga's gay scene, this is a café by day and bar by night. It also offers breakfasts, light snacks and tapas. It hosts regular events, from art exhibitions and film screenings to theme parties.

➕ d1 (fold-out map) ✉ Plaza de la Merced 16 ☎ 952 60 39 48 🕐 Daily 9–3

CAFÉ CON LIBROS

A relaxed, boho-chic café with a delightful terrace on the central Plaza de la Merced, this serves juices, shakes, salads and crêpes. It's a great spot to enjoy an evening drink and watch the world go by.

➕ d1 (fold-out map) ✉ Plaza de la Merced 19 ☎ 952 21 51 89 🕐 Mon–Fri 11am–1am, Sat–Sun 11am–2am

CAMPO DE GOLF GUADALHORCE

www.guadalhorce.com
Designed by Kosti Kuronen, this course is 7km (4 miles) from Málaga airport. There are two 9-hole greens in different styles: the second, with elevated greens and water obstacles, is the most demanding.

➕ Off map ✉ Carretera Cártama km 7, Campanillas ☎ 952 17 93 78

CAMPO DE GOLF REAL CLUB DE CAMPO DE MÁLAGA

www.rccm-golf.com
A very attractive course set in landscaped gardens and offering beautiful sea views. Attached to the Málaga Golf Parador, it's about a ten-minute drive from Málaga airport.

➕ H6 ✉ Autovía A7 Málaga-Algeciras, salida (exit) Coin km 231 ☎ 952 37 66 77

WHERE TO GO

The best areas for bars in Málaga are the Plaza de la Merced and Plaza del Marqués Vado Maestre, popularly known as Plaza Mijana. These squares, especially Plaza Mijana, are especially lively at weekends, when the terraces teem with well-dressed young locals, who gather here before moving on to the many nightclubs in the centre. For the best seafront nightclubs, head to the suburb of Pedregalejo.

CASANOVA LOUNGE CLUB

www.discotecasenmalaga.es/casanova/
One of the hottest places in town with chic, minimalist decor and displays on plasma screens where you can see music clips. It starts off mellow, but things hot up in the evenings when DJs play Latin House and R'n'B.

➕ c1 (fold-out map) ✉ Calle Luis de Velázquez 5 ☎ 952 22 49 07 🕐 Mon–Thu 4pm–3.30am, Fri–Sun 6pm–4.30am

INDIANA

An intimate bar dedicated to some of the most important rock groups of the last few decades. Decoration includes CDs, pictures and vinyls of legendary groups such as the Beatles, the Rolling Stones and Elvis Presley.

➕ c1 (fold-out map) ✉ Calle Nosquera 12 ☎ 952 60 94 37 🕐 Thu–Sat 10pm–4am

LEVEL

www.antimeditation.com
Start the night off with a drink in this stylish, minimally decorated bar, which is one of the best places in the city for local DJ sessions.

➕ c1 (fold-out map) ✉ Calle Beatas 10 ☎ 615 21 48 90 🕐 Wed–Thu 10pm–3am, Sat–Sun 10pm–4am

LICEO

The Lyceum is one of the city's biggest discos

dedicated to house music. It's located in an old, two-storey mansion with several bars and dance floors playing different music.

➕ c1 (fold-out map) ✉ Calle Beatas 2 ☎ 952 60 24 40 🕐 Thu–Sat 7pm–3am

EL NAVEGANTE

This is one of numerous bars with outdoor terraces on the Paseo Marítimo, overlooking the beach. With its nautically themed décor and comfy outdoor sofas, it's a popular spot in the city on hot summer nights, particularly with a slightly older crowd.

➕ d4 (fold-out map) ✉ Paseo Marítimo, Ciudad de Melilla 15 ☎ 952 20 63 48 🕐 Bar times vary

ONDA PASADENA

This attractive bar is one of the best places in town for a relaxed drink, and also hosts live gigs on Tuesday (usually jazz, but sometimes pop) and Thursday, which features flamenco.

➕ d1 (fold-out map) ✉ Calle Gómez Pallete 5 ☎ No phone 🕐 Daily 10pm–6am

SALA WENGE

One of the most exclusive clubs in central Málaga, this has two imposing doormen at the entrance so make sure you are dressed to impress or you won't make it on to the red carpet. Be prepared to queue.

➕ c1 (fold-out map) ✉ Calle Santa Lucía 11 ☎ No phone 🕐 Wed–Fri 10pm–6am, Sat–Sun 10pm–7am

SKOPAS

www.discotecasenmalaga.es/skopas/

This nightclub has been going strong for more than a decade and offers a guaranteed fun night out. It's one of the liveliest nightspots in the city.

➕ c1 (fold-out map) ✉ Louis Granados 6 ☎ 617 41 59 93 🕐 Sun–Thu 11pm–3.30am, Fri–Sat 11pm–4.30am

TEATRO CERVANTES

www.teatrocervantes.com

This theatre has a wide-ranging programme that includes everything from classical drama to musicals and children's theatre. It's home to the Philharmonic Orchestra

---

NIGHTCLUB ETIQUETTE

All the smart nightclubs in Málaga have strict dress codes, enforced by bouncers. Trainers and sports clothes are generally frowned upon. Note that entrance to most clubs is usually free from midnight until 2 or 3am, when bars and pubs close, and people surge into the clubs. Admission prices vary, but are usually between €5–€10. Hang on to your entrance ticket, which usually entitles you to a free drink.

---

and is also a popular venue for pop, jazz and classical concerts. The summer festival (July) is excellent. The adjoining Bar Cervantes is perfect for pre-theatre drinks.

➕ c1 (fold-out map) ✉ Calle Ramos Marín s/n ☎ Ticket line 902 36 02 95; information 952 22 41 00

LA TORTUGA

This is the most famous of the beachfront night-clubs in the Pedregalejo suburb, a short bus ride from the city. In summer, its much sought-after terrace fills up with young people, both Spanish and foreign, enjoying cocktails and Latin rhythms.

➕ Off map ✉ Paseo Marítimo el Pedregal 48 ☎ No phone 🕐 Daily 1pm–3am 🚌 L-34 (Bolivia)

TRIFÁSICO

www.trifasico.com

A lively cocktail bar, this is famous for its excellent *mojitos*. Every Thursday there is live music—from folk, jazz, tango to rock 'n' roll from the 1960s.

➕ c1 (fold-out map) ✉ Calle Beatas 9 ☎ 637 77 35 77 🕐 Daily 11pm–4am

ZZ PUB

www.zzpub.es

A classic, long-established rock bar, this hosts regular live rock concerts performed by local bands.

➕ c1 (fold-out map) ✉ Calle Tejón y Rodríguez 6 ☎ 952 44 15 95 🕐 Daily 10.30pm–3am

Restaurants

PRICES

Prices are approximate, based on a 3-course meal for one person.
€€€   over €45
€€   €25–€45
€   under €25

ANTIGUA CASA DE GUARDIA (€)

www.antiguacasadeguardia.net
This old-fashioned, barrel-lined tavern was founded in 1840 and offers a variety of local wines and seafood tapas.
🔹 b2 ✉ Alameda Principal 18 ☎ No phone 🕐 Tue–Fri 9am–10pm, Sat–Sun 10am–10pm

ASAKO (€€)

www.restauranteasako.com
Minimalist decoration and chill-out music provide a chic backdrop at Asako, where Japanese meets Mediterranean cuisine.
🔹 c1 (fold-out map) ✉ Calle Carretería 96 ☎ 952 21 40 60 🕐 Lunch and dinner; closed Sun

CAFÉ CENTRAL (€)

www.cafecentralmalaga.com
Join the Malagueños tucking into a hearty breakfast of *churros con chocolate*. Traditional Spanish fare, *churros* are made of sweet dough, deep fried, and eaten dipped in hot chocolate.
🔹 c1 (fold-out map) ✉ Plaza de la Constitución, 11 ☎ 952 22 49 72 🕐 Daily 8am–midnight

CAÑADU (€€)

The specialty at this cosy and central veggie restaurant is couscous with vegetables. On Friday, dinner is accompanied by a cello and piano concert. It's small and very popular, so book in advance.
🔹 d1 (fold-out map) ✉ Plaza de la Merced 21 ☎ 952 22 90 56 🕐 Daily lunch and dinner

EL CHINITAS (€€)

www.elchinitas.com
A long-established and much-loved classic, the interior is decorated with bullfighting and flamenco motifs. It's popular with visiting celebrities and is famous for local classics such as gazpacho and *tortilla de camarones* (Spanish omelette prepared with tiny prawns). It is best to book in advance.
🔹 c2 ✉ Calle Moreno Monroy 4 ☎ 952 21 09 72 🕐 Daily lunch and dinner

MÁLAGA DULCE

Málaga, formerly a raffish port city, was once full of barrel-lined wine cellars, which served the local sweet wine *Málaga Dulce* along with a range of simple tapas. A few survive (notably the Antigua Casa de Guardia, ▷ above), and they are well worth seeking out for a taste of old Málaga. But watch out: *Málaga Dulce* may slip down smoothly, but it packs an unexpected punch.

CITRON (€€)

An unusual restaurant offering a unique fusion of Oriental, Italian and Scandinavian cuisine. Try the salad with grilled goat's cheese or the duck with pineapple and mango chutney and finish up with the chocolate brownie.
🔹 d1 (fold-out map) ✉ Plaza de la Merced 10 ☎ 952 22 63 99 🕐 Daily 1.30–12.30

CLANDESTINO (€)

Tucked down a little back street, this popular restaurant doesn't take bookings and can be spotted by the queues at the door. Good-value, tasty Italian and Mediterranean cooking is the draw.
🔹 c1 (fold-out map) ✉ Calle Niño de Guevara 3 ☎ 952 21 93 90 🕐 Daily 1pm–1am

COMOLOCO (€)

Get here early to ensure a seat—this is one of the most popular places in town. Delicious pita bread sandwiches and salads at bargain prices mean it is always packed out.
🔹 c1 (fold-out map) ✉ Calle Dennis Belgrado 17 ☎ 952 21 65 71 🕐 Daily 1–4.30, 8–midnight

ERWAYA (€)

Tucked away near the cathedral in the old quarter, this pleasant little café-cum-bookshop is a wonderful place to while away an hour or two. You

can browse through the arty books on offer, while enjoying tea and cakes. If there's something you particularly like among the books, CDs and movies displayed, it can be purchased. All kinds of events are organized, including film screenings, storytelling, art exhibitions and more.

🔲 c2 ✉ Calle Afligidos 3 ☎ 952 60 85 99 🕓 Tue–Fri 10.30–2, 5–11, Sat–Sun 10.30–2, 5–11.30

IL LABORATORIO (€€)

A fashionable spot for breakfast, lunch and dinner, this offers tasty Italian favourites, with a special emphasis on homemade pasta. There's also a pleasant terrace.

🔲 c1 (fold-out map) ✉ Plaza San Pedro de Alcántara ☎ 952 22 49 98 🕓 Mon–Fri 8am–1am, Sat–Sun 10am–1am

LECHUGA (€)

With a perfect location on the central Plaza de la Merced, Lechuga is good for a quick bite. Sample sophisticated tapas, or a salad prepared with imaginative ingredients.

🔲 d1 (fold-out map) ✉ Plaza de la Merced 1 ☎ 610 39 14 94 🕓 Daily 1.30pm–12.30am

MARIANO (€€€)

This prestigious restaurant enjoys a fine reputation for its classic Andaluz cuisine. This includes everything from regional

hams and cured meats, to seafood, local *pescadito frito* (small fried fish) and steaks. Good wine list. Book in advance.

🔲 c1 (fold-out map) ✉ Plaza del Carbón 3 ☎ 952 12 18 58 🕓 Daily lunch and dinner

MIGUELITO EL CARIÑOSO (€€)

Sit on the seafront terrace and enjoy local specialties like *pescadito frito*, grilled sardines and delectable paella. The very reasonable prices mean that it's always full, so try to book before going.

🔲 Off map ✉ Paseo Maritimo El Pedregal 77 ☎ 952 29 94 43 🕓 Daily lunch and dinner 🚌 Bus L-34 (stop at Bolivia)

EL PALACETE (€€€)

www.elpalacetemalaga.com This deeply romantic restaurant is housed in

---

NON-STOP COOKING

Traditionally, visitors from other countries have had to get used to later Spanish dining hours along the Costa del Sol, or rely on tapas to fill the gap before dinner. But recently, a new trend for all-day kitchens has begun in some of the newer, fashionable establishments, meaning that you can wander in at any time and enjoy a full meal. Look out for signs saying *'cocina abierta todo el día'*.

---

a beautiful 17th-century mansion. Enjoy sophisticated regional cuisine in a charming setting—the best tables are out on the prettily tiled, plant-filled patio.

🔲 d1 (fold-out map) ✉ Calle Álamos 38 ☎ 952 22 09 88 🕓 Lunch and dinner; closed Sun dinner

PALACIO WOK (€€)

www.palaciowok.es The Asian trend has taken its time to hit Spain, but now there are wok restaurants everywhere. Choose your ingredients and see them cooked up in front of you. A good family option.

🔲 c2 ✉ Calle Molino Lario 13 ☎ 952 22 62 64 🕓 Daily lunch and dinner

EL PIMPI (€)

Located in the former stables of the Palacio Buenavista (now home to the Museo Picasso), this legendary bar attracts directors, writers and musicians. Settle down on a wooden bench with a bottle of local wine and a selection of tapas.

🔲 d2 ✉ Calle Granada 62 ☎ 952 22 89 90 🕓 Daily noon–2am

EL PIPEO (€€)

Just off the popular Plaza del Merced, this charming restaurant is a great place to try classic Mediterranean dishes such as home-made *croquetas* and *bacalao*

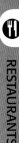

gratinado (grilled cod with a bubbling crust), so beloved by the locals.
🔼 d2 ✉ Calle Alcazabilla, 14 ☎ 952 21 17 81 🕐 Mon–Sat 9am–2am

PIZZERIA TRASTEVERE (€)

Close to the bullring, this Italian restaurant has some of the best pizzas in Málaga but you can also try delicious pasta dishes. There is a summer terrace.
🔼 e3 ✉ Avenida Canovas del Castillo 10 ☎ 952 21 90 80 🕐 Daily lunch and dinner

RETRUQUE (€€)

www.retruque.com
Modern and stylish, Retruque is a restaurant that offers a wide-ranging menu, which includes Mediterranean and Castillian dishes. Among its specialties are succulent dorado baked in a rock-salt crust, and grilled lamb chops.
🔼 Off map ✉ Avenida Pintor Joaquín Sorolla 36 ☎ 952 22 00 35 🕐 Daily lunch and dinner

SALMOREJO (€€)

www.salmorejotapas.es
For fresh, imaginative Andalucian cuisine with an original touch, try Salmorejo. The menu features everything from *tablas* (platters) of local cheeses and charcuterie, to Iberian steaks and fresh seafood. Live music (usually flamenco) on Thursday nights.

🔼 c2 ✉ Calle Fresca 12 ☎ 952 22 83 24 🕐 Lunch and dinner; closed Sun dinner

SOSÚA (€€)

Mediterranean favourites along with Dominican specialties are on offer here. Fish dishes, in particular the prawns in coconut sauce, are especially recommended.
🔼 d2 ✉ Calle Niño de Guevara 4 ☎ 952 21 04 69 🕐 Daily lunch and dinner

TABERNA EL TRASIEGO (€)

A handy central option, this old-fashioned tavern offers everything from sand-wiches and light snacks to tapas and more substantial fare. Prices are reasonable. Complement your meal with a good cava.
🔼 c2 ✉ Calle Santa Maria 23 ☎ 952 22 34 54 🕐 Mon–Sat 12pm–2am, Sun 12pm–5pm

---

SPECIAL DISH

Málaga is famous through-out Spain for its *pescadito frito*, also known as *frito Malagueño*. This is a platter with a varied selection of small, battered, deep-fried fish. The restaurants along the Paseo Maritimo in the beachside suburb of El Pedregal are especially known for *frito Malagueño*. While you are here, you should also try the *espeto de sardinas*–barbecued sardines served on a skewer.

EL TINTERO (€)

For a classic Malagueño experience, come to this old-fashioned seafront establishment in the El Palo neighbourhood. Waiters carry platters of freshly fried fish aloft, shouting out what is on offer. Diners pick whatev-er looks good, rather than ordering conventionally from a menu.
🔼 Off map ✉ Carretera de Almeria 99, El Palo ☎ 952 20 68 26 🕐 Daily lunch and dinner 🚌 Bus L-34 (stop at Bolivia)

EL VEGETARIANO DE LA ALCAZABILLA (€€)

Vegetarian and vegan salads, soups, main dishes and imaginative desserts are served at this pretty little restaurant, decorated with plants and colourful tiles.
🔼 c2 ✉ Calle Pozo del Rey 5 ☎ 952 21 48 58 🕐 Lunch and dinner; closed Sun

VINO MIO (€€)

www.restaurantevinomio.com
Warmly decorated with yellow-painted walls and wooden tables, this restaurant offers a surprisingly adventurous menu. Try Dundee's Delight–South American crocodile with pepper chutney. More conven-tional fare is available, along with tapas, and also a vegetarian selection.
🔼 d1 (fold-out map) ✉ Calle Alamos 11 ☎ 952 60 90 93 🕐 Daily 1.30pm–1am

From glittering resorts such as Puerto Banús to family-favourites like Torremolinos, this area also encompasses the Andalucian hinterland, including the great cities of Sevilla and Córdoba and tiny white villages.

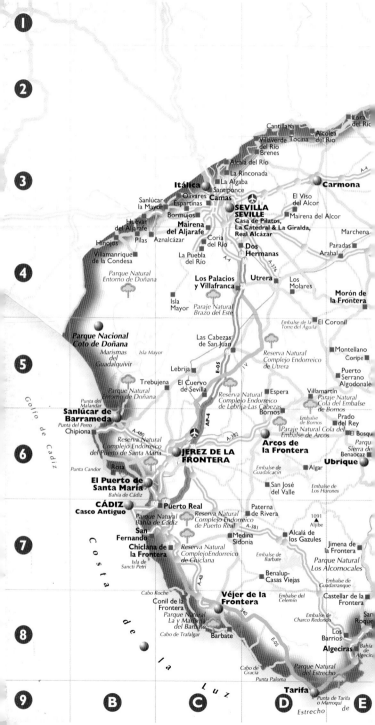

CÓRDOBA
La Mezquita,
Palacio de Viana

El Carpio

Almodóvar
del Río

Posadas

Guadalcázar

eñaflor

Palma
del Río

Fuente
Palmera

La Victoria

Fernán
Núñez

Espejo

Cañada
Rosal

San Sebastián de
los Ballesteros

La Carlota

Montemayor

La Campana

La Luisiana

Écija

Santaella

La Rambla

Montalbán
de Córdoba

Montilla

Fuentes de
Andalucía

Espacio Natural
Laguna de Zoñar

Aguilar de
la Frontera

Monturque

Reserva Natural
Laguna del Tiscar

Espacio Natural
Laguna del Rincón

Moriles

Lucena

La Lantejuela

El Rubio

Marinaleda

Puente
Genil

Reserva Natural
Complejo Endorreico
de La Lentejuela

Herrera

Reserva Natural
Laguna de los Jarales

Encinas
Reales

Embalse de
Iznájar

Estepa

Casariche

Badolatosa

Osuna

Aguadulce

Lora de
Estepa

Benamejí

Cuevas de
San Marcos

a Puebla
e Cazalla

Gilena

Pedrera

La Roda de
Andalucía

Palenciana

Cuevas
Bajas

Villanueva
de Algaidas

Reserva Natural
Laguna del Gosque

Sierra de
Yeguas

Alameda

Embalse de la
Puebla de Cazalla

Fuente de
Piedra

Mollina

Archidona

Los Corrales

Martín
de la Jara

Humilladero

Laguna Fuente
de Piedra

Reserva Natural
Peñón de Zaframagón

El Saucejo

Campillos

Reserva Natural
Lagunas de Campillos

Almargen

Antequera

Algámitas

Teba

Embalse de
Guadalhorce

Parque Natural El
Torcal de Antequera

Pruna

Cañete la Real

Embalse de
Guadalteba

Valle de
Abdalajís

Olvera

Torre-Alháquime

Alcalá
del Valle

Embalse del Conde
de Guadalhorce

Paraje Natural Desfiladero
de los Gaitanes

ahara de la
erra

El Gastor

Setenil

Cuevas
del Becerro

Ardales

Carratraca

Carratraca

Embalse de
Zahara-El Gastor

Arriate

El Burgo

Álora

Almogía

Grazalema

Montejaque

Ronda

Casarabonela

Pizarra

Natural
razalema

Benaoján

Ronda

Parque Natural
Sierra de las Nieves

Yunquera

Cártama

Villaluenga
del Rosario

1919
Torrecilla

Alozaina

ortes de la
rontera

Atajate

Serranía

Igualeja

Tolox

Guaro

Coín

Monda

Alhaurín
de la Torre

Alhaurín
El Grande

Torremolinos

Benadalid

Pujerra

Istán

Ojén

Mijas

Benalmádena

Algatocín

Jubrique

Punta Negra

Benarrabá

Benahavís

Fuengirola

araje Natural
Reales de
erra Bermeja

Gaucín

1449
Reales

Marbella

Punta de la Calaburra

Casares

Estepona

Puerto
Banús

Ensenada
de Marbella

Manilva

Costa del Sol

Punta de la Chullera

Punta Mala

La Línea de
la Concepción

Gibraltar

GB

Punta de
Europa

Gibraltar

N

0   20 km

0   10 miles

F   G   H

Cádiz: Casco Antiguo

The striking cathedral in Cádiz (left); interior of the church of San Felipe Neri (right)

THE BASICS

www.cadiz.es

🚇 B7

🍽 Numerous cafés, bars and restaurants

🚌 Bus connections from all major Spanish cities

🚆 Cádiz

♿ Few

💰 Admission to monuments varies

ℹ️ Paseo de Canalejas s/n, tel 956 24 10 01; Mon–Fri 8.30–6, Sat–Sun and public hols 9–5

HIGHLIGHTS

● Cathedral
● Picking up picnic supplies at the market
● Museo de Bellas Artes
● Museo de Cádiz
● Views from the Camera Obscura, Torre Tavira
● Plaza de la Mina
● Basking in the sun at Playa La Caleta

Piled up on an isthmus jutting toward Africa, Cádiz's piquant old quarter is imbued with a special light. Many monuments have been recently restored, but the anarchic mayhem around the market will transport you to the medina of old.

Square and monuments Charming squares are linked by a neat grid of narrow streets lined with appealingly battered houses. The grandest squares are dominated by the city's most important monuments, such as the frilly, baroque cathedral and the Mudéjar-style Teatro de la Falla. The Plaza de la Mina, the city's loveliest square, is overlooked by the excellent Museo de Cádiz, with paintings, archaeological findings and more.

Curiosities For the best views of the city, visit the camera obscura in the Torre Tavira, where a special pinhole camera reflects a 360-degree view of the city back onto a spherical canvas—kids love it. During the spectacular Carnival (held in February or March), the whole city comes alive with colourful parades, traditional singing and dancing, and street parties. Pick up picnic supplies at the chaotic and atmospheric market, where stallholders bellow their wares to the crowds.

Beaches Playa de la Victoria, in the new part of town, is the most popular beach, but the old quarter boasts lovely La Caleta, a glorious curving bay dotted with brightly painted boats, which is guarded at either end by squat castles, just the perfect spot for a day at the beach.

Córdoba

Graced with palm trees and flanked by water, the Alcázar is a highlight of Córdoba

Córdoba, along with Sevilla and Granada, forms the great triumverate of Andalucian cities, former capitals of Al-Andalus. Here, the fusion of Christian and Islamic traditions is most clearly felt, magnificently embodied in the vast Mezquita.

The old quarter The heart of old Córdoba is a whitewashed warren of narrow streets, overflowing with the bright blooms of bougainvillea, geraniums and jasmine. It's dominated by the enormous Mezquita (▷ 44–45), the largest and most extraordinary mosque in the Muslim world. On the banks of the river stand the remnants of a lavish palace, still known by its Arabic name: the Alcázar. A beautiful Mudéjar synagogue, built in the 14th century, survives in the enchanting former Jewish quarter, the Judería. Don't miss the Palacio de Viana (▷ 46), a resplendent 14th-century palace, celebrated for its beautiful patios.

Museums There are several excellent museums in Córdoba, including the Museo Arqueológico, in an elegant Renaissance building, and the Museo de Julio Romero de Torres, dedicated to the celebrated Córdoban artist.

Medina Azahara The tourist office arranges guided visits to the haunting site of Medina Azahara, 5km (3 miles) west of Córdoba. Almost nothing survives of what was once one of the grandest and most glittering palaces in all Al-Andalus, but the columns and arches, long stripped of their gold and marble, are poignant reminders of past glory.

THE BASICS

🔲 G1
🍴 Numerous cafés, bars and restaurants
🚌 Bus connections from all major Spanish cities
🚉 Córdoba
♿ Few
🎫 Admission varies
ℹ️ Calle Rey Heredia 22 (at temporary address at time of writing, new location not yet established), tel 902 20 17 74; Mon–Fri 8.30–2.30. There is also a tourist information kiosk at Plaza de Tendillas 4; daily 10–2, 4.30–7.30

HIGHLIGHTS

● Mezquita
● La Judería (Jewish quarter)
● Calleja de las Flores (famous flower-filled street)
● Alcázar
● Palacio de Viana
● Museo Arqueológico

Córdoba: La Mezquita

HIGHLIGHTS

● Patio de los Naranjos
● Mihrab
● Capilla de Villaviciosa
● Capilla Real
● Dome

TIP

● Entrance to the Mezquita is free every day between 8.30am–10am. This is also a good time to visit in order to avoid the crowds.

One of the largest and most splendid mosques ever built, Córdoba's Mezquita continues to dazzle after 12 centuries. Despite its reconsecration as a Catholic cathedral, its forest of horseshoe arches survive remarkably unchanged.

History of a mosque Abd-ar-Rahman I, the first Emir of Córdoba, built his great mosque over the remnants of a 5th-century Visigothic basilica, which, in turn, was constructed over a Roman temple. Work began on the Mezquita in 784, which was expanded by subsequent rulers until it became the second-largest mosque in the Muslim world. After the Christian Reconquest of Córdoba of 1236, when Frederick III of Castile recaptured the city, the Mezquita was converted into a Catholic cathedral, a position it still maintains.

Clockwise from left: Córdoba's splendid mosque, La Mezquita; the stunning interior of the mosque; outstanding Moorish architecture is a feature of the mosque; the courtyard of the mosque; a detail from the mosque's Puerta del Perdon (Gateway of Forgiveness)

The Mezquita Entrance to the Mezquita is through the Patio de los Naranjos, a wide square still planted with orange trees that elegantly echo the sea of horseshoe arches within. The arches are supported by more than 850 columns, beautifully worked in marble, jasper and granite. The crowning jewel of the Mezquita is the Mihrab, the niche that denotes the direction of Mecca. The nearby Capilla de Villaviciosa and Capilla Real are both later Christian additions.

The cathedral The Mezquita was reconsecrated as a Christian cathedral in 1236, but, unusually for the times, its architecture was largely left intact. This changed in the 16th century, when a classic Renaissance nave was dropped into the centre of the complex. Fortunately, the Mezquita is so big that this curious insertion goes almost unnoticed.

THE BASICS

✚ G1
✉ Patio de los Naranjos
☎ 957 47 05 12
🕐 May–end Sep Mon–Sat 8.30am–7pm, Sun 8.30–10.15, 2–7; Oct–end Apr closes one hour earlier (times may vary)
🍴 Numerous cafés and restaurants
♿ Few
💰 Moderate
❓ Mass is held at 11am on Sun

45

Córdoba: Palacio de Viana

The courtyard of the Viana palace bedecked with flowers (left); decorative tiles (right)

THE BASICS

🔲 G1

✉ Plaza de San Gome 2

☎ 957 49 67 41

🕐 Oct–end May Mon–Fri 10–1, 4–6, Sat 10–1; Mid-Jun–end Sep Mon–Sat 9–2; closed early Jun–mid-Jun (for two weeks)

🍴 Numerous cafés and restaurants nearby but not in the palace

♿ None

💷 Moderate; garden-only ticket inexpensive

❓ If you don't want to visit the palace interior, admission tickets just for the gardens are also available at a reduced price

HIGHLIGHTS

● Patios
● Garden
● Galería de los Azulejos
● Salón de las Artes
● Library

This austerely beautiful palace, formerly home to the Marquises of Viana, was begun in the 14th century. Extensively remodelled and enlarged over the centuries, it is set around more than a dozen exquisite patios and overlooks a luxuriant 18th-century garden.

The interior The opulent interior is at once palatial and intimate, and has been beautifully restored to provide a glimpse into life in an aristocratic home. Some of the original decoration of the interior dates back to the 17th and 18th centuries and includes some beautiful French and Spanish furnishings, tapestries, porcelain and silverwork. The Galería de los Azulejos boasts an original Roman mosaic floor (it's thought the palace was built over a Roman villa) and contains a fine collection of Mudéjar and Renaissance ceramics from the 13th century onwards. The Salón de las Artes is adorned with lavish murals but the highlight is undoubtedly the magnificent library, with more than 7,000 historic volumes.

Patios and garden The central patio is at the very heart of domestic life, a cool, flower-scented retreat that is deliberately hidden from public view. The Palacio de Viana boasts the most beautiful patios in the city. The flower-filled squares, a riot of green fronds and bright blooms, are a sheer delight. Linked by covered galleries, and dotted with pretty stone fountains, they provide the city with one of its most magical corners. The attractive historic garden is an 18th-century design.

Estepona

A former fishing village, now a popular resort, Estepona is one of the largest towns on the Costa del Sol. Set in a fertile valley planted with citrus trees and exotic fruit, it boasts more than 20km (12 miles) of blissful sandy beaches and has good facilities for sports and activities.

The old town Estepona's tiny old quarter is a pretty little jumble of cobbled streets, which loop between a sprinkle of delightful squares. Look out for the pink-and-white Torre de Reloj (Clocktower), which overlooks the square of the same name, and stop for a drink on the Plaza de las Flores, dotted with orange trees. Part of a 16th-century castle, built by order of the Catholic Kings to defend against pirates, and a charming little church, the 18th-century Iglesia de Nuestra Señora de los Remedios, are among the best surviving monuments.

The port, beaches and the park Estepona still has a small fishing fleet, and the sight of the trawlers returning at dawn to offload their catch is unforgettable. There are boats of a very different kind in the marina, where gleaming yachts are overlooked by popular bars and restaurants. The long beaches stretch in either direction, all well equipped with everything from snack bars (*chiringuitos*) to sun loungers. The main beach, La Rada, is right in front of the town and is the most popular. Best for families is the El Cristo beach, just to the west. Don't forget to visit the Parque de los Pedregales, especially if you have children, where you can hike and ride on bikes or horses.

THE BASICS

www.estepona.es/turismo

🔼 F7

🍴 Numerous cafés, bars and restaurants

🚌 Bus connections with Málaga, Marbella and along the Costa del Sol

🚆 Nearest train station is at Fuengirola

♿ Good

ℹ Avda San Lorenzo 1, tel 952 80 20 02

HIGHLIGHTS

● Strolling around the old quarter
● Watching the dawn fish auction at the port
● A sunset drink at the marina
● Views from Parque de los Pedregales
● *Pescadito frito* (fried fish) on the beach

Jerez de la Frontera

HIGHLIGHTS

● A tapas tour of the taverns
● Dressage performance at the Real Escuela Andaluza del Arte Ecuestre
● Flamenco show at a *peña*
● Sherry tasting at a historic bodega

TIP

● Many bodegas require reservations in advance, especially the smaller wineries, so visitors are advised to contact the tourist office for information before arrival.

Jerez is the cradle of flamenco and the home of sherry. It's a modest little city, with few monuments, but its traditional taverns and *peñas* (flamenco groups) lend it a piquant and deeply authentic charm.

Bodegas Sherry, historically known as 'sack', has been made here for centuries, and the Jerez–Cádiz area was the first Spanish wine region to gain D.O. status (see www.sherry.org for more information). Several bodegas have opened their doors to visitors: among the best-known of these are Tío Pepe, Harvey and Sandeman. The tourist office has a full list of bodegas with opening hours and contact details, and many of these bodegas are included in the region's 'Ruta del Vino de Jerez' (details at the tourist office). As well as sherry, the city is also famous for brandy and Jerez wine vinegar.

Clockwise from top left: ready to perform at the Real Escuela Andaluza del Arte Ecuestre in Jerez; old Jerez street; try and catch a flamenco show; wine barrel signed by Sir Winston Churchill; the 11th-century Alcázar displays fine Moorish architecture; Jerez is the home of Spanish sherry

Equestrian displays Jerez is also renowned for horses, and numerous local ranches breed the elegant Andalucian horse, long the preferred mount of the kings of Spain. They are one of the oldest breeds in the world, and are often used in dressage. You can see these beautiful animals perform at the Fundación Real Escuela Andaluza del Arte Ecuestre (www.realescuela.org), which hosts extraordinary equestrian shows (Mar–29 Dec Tue, Thu and Fri 12pm, Fri only in Aug). There is also a museum dedicated to the art of dressage.

Flamenco Flamenco is the city's soundtrack, its syncopated rhythms and haunting melodies echo on every street and square. There are numerous flamenco shows (*tablaos*) geared toward tourists. In late February/early March, the city erupts with the fabulous International Flamenco Festival.

THE BASICS

www.turismojerez.com
🚩 C6
🍴 Numerous cafés, bars and restaurants
🚌 Bus connections from all major Spanish cities
🚉 Jerez
♿ Few
ℹ Alameda Cristina, Edificio Los Claustros, tel 956 34 17 11

Marbella

TOP 25

HIGHLIGHTS

- Marbella's old town
- Patio de los Naranjos
- Plaza de la Iglesia
- The evening stroll along the seafront promenade
- Marina

TIP

- For a taste of the high life, head to one of the exclusive beach clubs and settle into a luxurious lounger with cocktail in hand.

Marbella, along with its suburb Puerto Banús (▷ 53), is the chicest resort on the Costa del Sol. The jet set hide away in their villas in the hills, but emerge to explore the enchanting old town, full of smart boutiques and galleries, or lounge at one of the exclusive beach clubs.

Casco Antiguo Marbella is beautifully nestled in a hollow formed by the surrounding Sierra Blanca, and its whitewashed old town is still partly enclosed by medieval walls. The Arabic heritage is once again evident in the sinuous streets lined with whitewashed villas. Along Calle Trinidad, you'll find the remnants of a 10th-century Arabic castle, of which just an arch and a few columns survive. At the centre is the Patio de los Naranjos, with a charming Renaissance fountain, overlooked

Clockwise from far left: take a wander round the streets of old Marbella; the resort of Marbella with the hills behind; holiday makers on the beach; take a trip around the town in a horse and carriage; lovely Marbella old town

by the 16th-century city hall, and the pretty little Ermita de Santiago. Just a few steps from here is a sprinkling of tiny squares, including the lovely Plaza de la Iglesia, overlooked by the modest baroque church of Nuestra Señora de la Encarnación.

The seafront The main town beaches, Playa de Venus and Playa de la Bajadilla, are curved along two bays, which link Marbella's pretty little fishing port and the glossy, yacht-filled marina. The long, sandy Playa de la Fontanilla (beyond the marina) and Playa El Fuerte (to the north) are the most fashionable and crowded beaches. A smart promenade, shaded with palm trees, lines the seafront and is a popular place for a pre-dinner stroll. Much of the city's nightlife is concentrated around the marina, where bars and clubs stay open until dawn during the summer months.

THE BASICS

www.marbella.es

➕ G7

🍴 Numerous cafés, bars and restaurants

🚌 Bus connections from Málaga and all other towns along the Costa del Sol

🚉 Nearest train station is at Fuengirola

♿ Good

ℹ Plaza de los Naranjos (central square), tel 952 82 35 50

Parque Natural El Torcal de Antequera

Strange geological formations (left); taking a hike through the park (right)

THE BASICS

➕ H5
✉ Carretera de Antequera–Vilanueva de la Concepión km 13
☎ 952 70 25 05
🕐 Call for details
🍴 Café
🚌 Nearest bus at Vilanueva de la Concepción
♿ Good in Interpretation Centre; few in park
💶 Free; inexpensive for observatory night visits

HIGHLIGHTS

● Wildflowers and discovering wild orchids
● Birds of prey and bird-watching
● Stone forms in shapes such as the Sphinx and the Toad
● Star gazing at the observatory
● Views from *Las Ventanillas* (little windows)

This park encompasses a landscape of surreal limestone rock forms, shaped by wind and time over more than 25 million years. Popular with hikers, botanists and bird-watchers, drawn by the beautiful scenery and the curious flora and fauna.

Hiking routes There are three signposted routes around the natural park. The easiest, marked in green, is a short 1.6km (1 mile) walk. More dramatic is the slighter longer yellow route (2.5km/1.5 miles), which passes some of the most famous of the extraordinary stone forms. The third route, marked in red, is only a little longer, at about 4.5km (3 miles), but is considerably less popular and gives hikers a better chance to spot wildlife.

Flora and fauna The landscape is arid and apparently inhospitable, and yet it manages to support a surprising variety of flora and fauna. Peonies, rock roses and other wildflowers dot the stones with bright splashes of colour, and holm oaks, hawthorn and maple provide tiny pockets of shade. There are numerous lizards and snakes, as well as foxes, badgers and the Spanish ibex (a kind of mountain goat). Circling high, you may spot sparrowhawks, kestrels, peregrines, griffon vultures and Bonelli's eagles.

Star-gazing The new Interpretation Centre includes one of the most advanced astronomical observatories in Spain. It offers special night visits; call for details.

Aimed at the rich and famous—it costs nothing to admire the yachts in the marina

Puerto Banús

Legendary playground of the rich and famous, Puerto Banús is Spain's most glamorous resort. The glittering marina is packed with glossy yachts, the streets are lined with designer shops, and the sleek bars and clubs have a strict door policy.

Port and beaches The port is the focus of the resort, which was constructed in 1968 as one of Spain's first purpose-built, village-style complexes. Ultra-luxurious, brilliant white apartments are clustered around the marina. The streets around the port are lined with smart restaurants, shops, bars and clubs, and the promenade is always thronged with people hoping for a glimpse of Antonio Banderas or football stars. The most sought-after restaurants and bars are on the front line of the port, but they are expensive. Explore the small streets around the port to find better bargains and less crowded surroundings. At night throngs of well-heeled visitors emerge from their Lamborghinis and Ferraris to flock to the exclusive bars and nightclubs. The long sandy Playa del Duque and Playa de Rio Verde to the south, and Playa Puerto Banús to the north, all offer excellent amenities but are crammed in high season.

Activities Puerto Banús offers every facility for watersports, from sailing to jet-skiing. It's also possible to charter a yacht with a skipper, for a truly glamorous experience. In the vicinity, you can go horse-riding and paragliding, and play tennis, football or squash. There are also luxurious hotels with fabulous day spas, if you fancy a day of pampering.

THE BASICS

www.marbella.es/turismo

⊞ F7

🍴 Numerous bars, cafés and restaurants

🚌 Bus connections from Málaga, Marbella and all towns along the Costa del Sol

🚆 Nearest train station is at Fuengirola

♿ Few

🛈 Accesso al Puerto (Poniente), tel 952 81 85 70

HIGHLIGHTS

● Window-shopping around the exclusive boutiques
● Renting a luxury car for a day
● A cocktail overlooking the port, admiring the yachts
● A night out at an exclusive club

Ronda

HIGHLIGHTS

● Views from Puente Nuevo
● Ambling through La Ciudad
● An evening stroll through the Alameda Tajo
● A drink on the terrace of the Ronda parador, overlooking the Puente Nuevo

TIP

● The Ronda region has recently gained prominence as a wine-growing area. Several bodegas open: ask at the tourist office for details.

In the rugged sierras behind the Costa del Sol, Ronda is breathtakingly set on either side of a steep gorge. A magnificent 18th-century stone bridge spans the gorge, affording stunning views over the elegant city and across the mountains.

La Ciudad The historic heart of Ronda is known simply as La Ciudad ('the city'), a tightly packed kernel of winding streets that follow the ancient pattern of the Arabic medina. At the Casa del Gigante ('the giant's house', named for some curious statues found in the ruins), the sparse remnants of a Nasrid-era palace can be explored. Elegant mansions and churches grew up after the Christian reconquest in the 15th century, including the handsome Palacio de Mondragón, which retains some exquisite arches from an earlier,

Clockwise from far left: the town of Ronda is spectacularly perched on a massive rocky outcrop; pretty iron balconies are a feature in the town; the incredible 15th-century bridge that divides Ronda's old and new buildings; aerial view of the countryside around the town; the bullring in Ronda

Arabic palace, and now houses the excellent Museo Municipal. Several other museums are clustered here, including the entertaining Museo del Bandolero (Bandit Museum) and the Museo Lara, with a quirky private collection of historic weapons and cameras plus much more. It hosts flamenco performances on Thursday evenings.

Puente Nuevo and the bullring The splendid, 18th-century Puente Nuevo spans the gorge, linking La Ciudad with the rest of the town. From the bridge, there are stupendous views of the hanging houses on the cliffs. In the newer part of town, which was largely laid out in the 18th century, is the historic bullring, one of the oldest and most beautiful in Spain. There's a small museum attached. For more magnificent views, take a stroll through the Alameda del Tajo, elegant 19th-century gardens.

THE BASICS

www.turismoderonda.es
F6
Numerous cafés, bars and restaurants
Bus links from Málaga
Ronda
Few
Paseo de Blas Infante s/n, tel 952 18 71 19

Sevilla

TOP
25

Details of tiles in the Plaza de España (left); a lovely arched bridge in the city (right)

THE BASICS

www.turismo.sevilla.org

➕ C3

🍴 Numerous cafés, restaurants and bars

🚌 Bus connections to Madrid and all major towns in Andalucía

🚃 Sevilla

♿ Few

ℹ️ Plaza del Triunfo 1-3, tel 954 21 00 05

HIGHLIGHTS

- Barrio Santa Cruz
- Casa de Pilatos
- Real Alcázar
- Cathedral and belltower
- Museo de Bellas Artes
- Maestranza bullring

TIP

- Sevilla's best shopping can be found on or near the Calle Sierpes. Nearby Calle Cuna is full of shops selling traditional flamenco outfits and accessories.

Sevilla (known in English as Seville) is the most beguiling of cities, curled sinuously on the banks of the River Guadalquivir and overlooked by the great minaret and belltower of La Giralda. For sheer romance, few cities can compare.

Barrio Santa Cruz Sevilla's former Jewish quarter, an alluring crooked maze of whitewashed lanes, is perfect for an aimless wander. Scarlet geraniums blaze from the balconies, and ornate wrought-iron gates offer glimpses into colourful, tiled patios. The Casa de Pilatos (▷ 57), still a private aristocratic home, is utterly enchanting, its ancient tiled salons overlooking a secret, flower-filled garden. Dominating the southern end is the hulking cathedral (▷ 58–59), topped by the winsome belltower, La Giralda, which has become the city's symbol. Beyond it is magnificent Real Alcázar, the Royal Palace (▷ 60–61), still used by the Spanish royal family when they visit Sevilla.

Museums and monuments The Museo de Bellas Artes has a splendid collection of paintings and sculpture. La Cartuja, in a secluded zone by the riverbank, has been resurrected as an excellent contemporary art gallery. Most works are exhibited in a modern annexe, but the ancient church is used for temporary exhibitions. Back in the old city centre, on the banks of the river, is the splendid 18th-century Maestranza bullring, considered the finest in Spain. Visit the delightfully eccentric Palacio de Lebrija, full of ancient finds collected by one of Spain's first female archaeologists.

Interior of the Casa de Pilatos (left); imposing statue on the patio of the palace (right)

TOP 25

Sevilla: Casa de Pilatos

This enchanting palace, still the main residence of the Dukes of Medinaceli, was begun at the end of the 15th century, and is an exquisite fusion of Renaissance and Mudéjar architecture. The magical little garden is an oasis of calm.

Gardens and patio A grand marble gateway, adorned with busts of Roman emperors and Spanish kings, announces the entrance to this remarkable palace, which opens into an expansive central patio. A series of chambers, beautifully tiled with traditional Mudéjar ceramics, are arranged around the patio, with delicate horseshoe arches framing sublime views of the flower-filled garden beyond. Some of these chambers were designed in the 16th century to display Greek and Roman antiquities, and still contain some fine antique sculptures.

The apartments The Ducal apartments are reached by a superb staircase, encrusted with sumptuous tiles and overlooked by a magnificent cupola. This staircase marks the transition from the grand, public space of the central patio to the intimate private apartments. These salons, executed between the 16th and 19th centuries, contain a fine array of paintings, tapestries and original furnishings from the Medinaceli collection. Many of these rooms boast richly gilded coffered ceilings, while others have delightful 16th-century murals and frescoes depicting mythological scenes by Francisco Pacheco (1564–1644), who moved to Sevilla at a very young age.

THE BASICS

www.fundacionmedinaceli.org

🔟 C3

✉ Plaza de Pilatos 1

☎ 954 22 52 98

🕐 Nov–end Mar daily 9–6; Apr–end Oct 9–7

🍴 Numerous restaurants and cafés nearby

🚌 Local bus services

🚉 Sevilla

♿ Few

🎟 Ground floor moderate; whole house moderate

HIGHLIGHTS

● Jardín Chico (little garden)
● Roman reliefs in ground floor chambers
● Tiled grand staircase
● Coffered ceilings in first floor apartments

Sevilla: La Catedral and La Giralda

Sevilla's enormous cathedral was built over the ruins of the 12th-century Great Mosque. The former Minaret was converted into the famous belltower, La Giralda. The cathedral's shadowy interior contains a dazzling altarpiece and fine artworks.

The exterior The trim patio with its neat rows of orange trees and the minaret, given a frothy Gothic belltower but otherwise intact, are all that survive of the Great Mosque. The belltower, called La Giralda, is the city's best-loved symbol, and can be climbed for spectacular views. The best of the Gothic portals are the Puerta del Bautismo and the Puerta de la Asunción, both encrusted with sculpture.

The interior This is the largest Gothic cathedral in the world, but its immensity only becomes

apparent once inside. The huge central nave contains a spectacular choir, flanked by gigantic organs, and culminates in the impressive main altar. This is decorated with a vast, 37m (120ft), Gothic altarpiece, which glitters with gold and is contained behind an elaborate grille. The Capilla Real contains the tombs of Saint Fernando, who conquered the city in 1248, and his son Alfonso the Wise. Look out for the surprisingly short tomb of Christopher Columbus (1451–1506), which may or may not contain his last remains. The Dominican Republic also claims the explorer's bones, which have yet to undergo DNA testing. The Sacristy contains the cathedral's treasures, which include paintings by Murillo and Zurbarán and a curious, if gory, collection of reliquaries, containing the rather gruesome bones, hair and nails of saints and martyrs.

THE BASICS

www.catedralsevilla.org
♼ C3
✉ Plaza Virgen de los Reyes
☎ 954 21 49 71
🕑 Jul–end Aug Mon–Sat 9.30–3.30, Sun and public hols 2.30–6; Sep–end Jun Mon–Sat 11–5, Sun and public hols 2.30–6
🍴 Numerous cafés, bars and restaurants nearby
♿ Good
💷 Moderate; free on Sun

Sevilla:
Real Alcázar

TOP 25

HIGHLIGHTS

- Salón de los Embajadores
- Salón de Justicia
- Patio de las Doncellas
- A concert in the gardens on a balmy summer night

TIP

- Book your ticket in advance in high season, when visitor numbers are limited. During the summer (end June to early Sep), concerts are held nightly in the romantic gardens.

The Real Alcázar is a fairytale royal palace first built by the Almohads. The finest section was constructed by Pedro the Cruel in the 14th century, an exotic Mudéjar complex of intricate stuccowork and iridescent tiles.

The Palacio Mudéjar Although very little survives of the original Almohad edifice, the palace built by Pedro the Cruel is a masterpiece of Mudéjar art, reminiscent of Granada's famous Alhambra. Visit the Salón de Justicia with its beautiful star-shaped coffered ceiling, and, just beyond it, framed by delicate horseshoe archways, the Patio de Yeso, virtually all that remains of the Almohad palace. On the other side of the courtyard, the Salón de los Embajadores is filled with intricate tilework of dazzling beauty. Beyond

Clockwise from far left: a dazzling sight—the interior of the Real Alcázar; decorative urn in the formal gardens of the palace; bird's-eye view of the palace; intricate detail of the splendid dome of the Ambassador's Hall; strolling in the gardens; more superb detail on the exterior of the palace

the main entrance, the Patio de las Doncellas is a stunning, extravagantly tiled courtyard with a fountain. Labyrinthine chambers lead off this courtyard, superbly decorated by the finest Muslim artists of the era. The Patio de las Muñecas (the Patio of the Dolls) was once the domestic heart of the palace, and legend has it that the two tiny faces on the base of one of the arches will bring luck—if you can spot them.

The Gothic palace After the delicacy and beauty of the Mudéjar palace, the later Gothic additions appear decidedly clumsy. The Catholic Kings added the Casa de Contratación, where the conquest of the Americas was planned, and, later, Charles V added several lofty salons, which now contain fine Flemish tapestries. Beyond them is the lovely garden with fountains and a small maze.

THE BASICS

www.patronato-
alcazarsevilla.es

✚ C3

✉ Plaza del Triunfo

☎ 954 50 23 24

🕐 Oct–end Mar Tue–Sun 9.30–5; Apr–end Sep 9.30–7

🍽 Café

♿ Few

💰 Moderate

Tarifa

TOP 25

A view of the 10th-century Moorish castle (left); Tarifa's harbour (right)

THE BASICS

- D9
- Numerous cafés, bars and restaurants
- Bus links from Algeciras, Málaga and Cádiz
- Nearest train station Algeciras
- Few
- Paseo la Alameda s/n, tel 956 68 09 93

HIGHLIGHTS

- A mint tea in one of old Tarifa's *teterías*
- Iglesia de San Mateo
- Learning to windsurf on the Playa de Tarifa
- Whale-watching trip
- The beach at Baelo Claudio

Tarifa sits right on the southernmost tip of Europe, gazing across the Straits to Africa, just 14km (9 miles) away. Tarifa's old town, a low huddle of whitewashed villas, splashed with bright blue, still feels distinctly Moorish.

The old town Still tucked behind white walls, Tarifa's old town is a delight to explore on foot. There are few monuments or famous sights, but the crooked little lanes with their pretty villas, tea shops and small boutiques are very appealing. The Castillo de Guzmán el Bueno (not open to the public) dominates the port, a 9th-century fortress that serves as a reminder that it was from Tarifa the North Africans began their conquest of the Iberian peninsula. The Iglesia de San Mateo is the grandest church, a late-Gothic edifice with a later baroque façade. There is plenty of nightlife, but the laid-back, bohemian crowd who are attracted to this drowsy town ensure that the pace remains slow and relaxing.

Beaches and activities The long, white-sand beaches stretch for several kilometres along the coast, and are hugely popular with windsurfers, kitesurfers and surfers. This is the windiest corner of Europe, and forests of wind machines whirl on the hills behind the town. There are numerous other activities available, including snorkelling, diving and horse-riding. Several organizations offer whale- and dolphin-watching trips, where sightings of schools of dolphins and the glossy black pilot whales are very common.

More to See

ANTEQUERA

www.antequera.es

In the foothills of the Sierra del Torcal, whitewashed Antequera is dominated by an Arabic fortress, which offers splendid views. Behind it rises the great crag of the Peña de los Enamorados (Lover's Rock), where legend recounts a Muslim girl and her Christian lover threw themselves in despair. The town is filled with elegant mansions and fine churches.
➕ H5 🍽 Cafés, restaurants, bars
♿ Few ℹ Plaza de San Sebastián 7, tel 952 70 25 05

ARCOS DE LA FRONTERA

www.ayuntamientoarcos.org

One of the prettiest *pueblos blancos* (white villages) in Andalucía, Arcos de la Frontera is piled dramatically on a craggy rock with a stunning mountain backdrop. The old quarter is breathtakingly lovely, and filled with elegant palaces and the perfect storybook castle.
➕ D6 🍽 Cafés, restaurants, bars ♿ Few
ℹ Plaza de Cabildo 2, tel 956 70 22 64

BENALMÁDENA

www.benalmadena.com

Benalmádena is a popular tourist resort located midway between Torremolinos and Fuengirola. Its Arabic roots are evident in the pretty little old quarter, set back from the coast. Families love the Parque de Atracciones Tívoli, with rollercoasters, carousel and more. A cable car links the coast with a spectacular mountain viewing-point.
➕ H6 🍽 Cafés, restaurants, bars ♿ Few
ℹ Avenida Antonio Machado 10, tel 952 44 24 94

CARMONA

www.turismo.carmona.org

Carmona is a graceful, tranquil town of whitewashed mansions, elegant churches and a splendid castle (now a *parador*). A roman necropolis and amphitheatre attest to its long history; this is one of the oldest settlements in Andalucía.
➕ D3 🍽 Cafés, restaurants, bars ♿ Few
ℹ Arco de la Puerta de Sevilla, s/n, tel 954 19 09 55

Rooftop view of Antequera

The Convent of Santa Clara in Carmona

CASARES

www.casares.es

A winding road twists up through the Sierra Bermeja and culminates in lofty Casares, a breathtaking tumble of low, whitewashed houses crowned by a Moorish castle. Explore the picturesque old quarter, and climb to the top of the castle for astounding views.

🟦 E7 🍴 Cafés, restaurants, bars ♿ Few
ℹ️ Calle Carrera s/n, tel 952 89 55 21

COSTA DE LA LUZ

The Atlantic coast between Tarifa and Cádiz has been christened the Costa de la Luz ('coast of light'). Considerably less developed than the Costa del Sol, its beautiful white sand beaches are wild and often windswept. Despite increasing popularity, the little resorts are more popular with locals than international visitors.

🟦 B7–D9

EL PUERTO DE SANTA MARÍA

www.elpuertosm.es

A handsome port town on the banks of the River Guadalete, El Puerto de Santa María boasts an atmospheric old quarter filled with aristocratic mansions, and celebrated restaurants and tapas bars. It's one of the main centres of sherry production, with numerous bodegas open to visitors.

🟦 B6 🍴 Cafés, restaurants, bars ♿ Few
ℹ️ Calle Luna 22, tel 956 54 24 75

FUENGIROLA AND TORREMOLINOS

www.fuengirola.org; www.ayto-torremolinos.org

Two of the most popular resorts on the Costa del Sol, Fuengirola and Torremolinos have long been synonymous with sun, fun, sea and sand on a budget. The long, sandy beaches are magnificent, and, while anonymous apartment blocks and modern hotels predominate along this strip of coast, Fuengirola still boasts a picturesque fishing port.

Fuengirola 🟦 H6/H7 🍴 Cafés, restaurants, bars ♿ Few ℹ️ Avda Jesús Santos Rein 6, Fuengirola, tel 952 46 07 58

Torremolinos 🟦 H6 🍴 Cafés, restaurants, bars ♿ Few ℹ️ Plaza Independencia s/n, Torremolinos, tel 952 37 42 31

Chugging past the statue of Christopher Columbus on the Costa de la Luz

The beach in Torremolinos (below); Plaza de la Constitución, Fuengirola (opposite)

GIBRALTAR

Piled around a great rock attached by a narrow isthmus to the Spanish mainland, Gibraltar is a British outpost, complete with red telephone boxes, fish-and-chip shops, and old-fashioned pubs. Take the cable car to the Top of the Rock for stunning views, and meet the famous apes at the Ape's Den near Europa Point. Dolphin trips are also available. Note that passports are required to go over the border into Gibraltar.

➕ E8 🍴 Cafés, restaurants, bars ♿ Few
ℹ Duke of Kent House, Cathedral Square, tel 956 77 49 50

GRAZALEMA

High in the Sierra de Grazalema, this pretty white village is beautifully set against a rugged backdrop of pine-clad mountains. It's an excellent base for hikers, with several great trails starting from the village. The wettest village in Spain, it offers a cool retreat during the scorching summer.

➕ E6 🍴 Limited cafes, restaurants, bars
♿ Few ℹ Plaza España 1, tel 956 13 22 25

ITÁLICA

Itálica, 7km (4 miles) from Sevilla, was founded in 206–205BC, making it one of the earliest Roman settlements on the Iberian peninsula. It is also one of the best preserved, with a particularly fine amphitheatre.

➕ C3 ✉ Avda de Extremadura 2, Santiponce ☎ 955 62 22 66 🕐 Oct–end Mar Tue–Sat 9–5.30, Sun 10–4; Apr–end Sep Tue–Sat 8.30–8.30, Sun and public hols 9–3
🍴 In Santiponce ♿ Few

OSUNA

An elegant university town occupying a panoramic position on a hillside overlooking the Sevillian plains, Osuna has several fine 16th-century monuments. Finest among them is the Colegiata, where the last remains of most of the Dukes of Osuna were laid in the Panteón de los Duques. The Convento de la Encarnación is prettily tiled with depictions of typical local scenes.

➕ F4 🍴 Cafés, restaurants, bars ♿ Few
ℹ Plaza Mayor s/n, tel 954 81 57 32

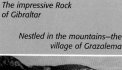

The impressive Rock of Gibraltar

Nestled in the mountains—the village of Grazalema

PARQUE NACIONAL COTO DE DOÑANA

One of the most impressive wetland reserves in Europe, with a wealth of bird and animal life, the Parque Nacional Coto de Doñana is an essential visit for all nature-lovers. Entrance to the protected areas is strictly controlled, but visits can be arranged through the main park information office.

✚ B5 ✉ Centro de Recepción El Acebuche, near El Rocío ☎ 959 43 96 29 🍴 Café at the visitors' centre ♿ Few

SANLÚCAR DE BARRAMEDA

www.aytosanlucar.org/turismo
At the mouth of the River Guadalquivir, this lively and historic little town is famous for its excellent bodegas, which produce delicious *manzanilla* (a kind of sherry), traditional tapas bars and beautiful sandy beaches. Don't miss the incredible horse-racing events along the beaches, which take place every August.

✚ B6 🍴 Cafés, restaurants, bars ♿ Few 🛈 Calle Calzada del Ejército, tel 956 36 61 10

UBRIQUE

www.ubrique.es
Nestled in the foothills of the Sierra Ubrique, this is one of the largest of the *pueblos blancos* in southern Andalucía's beautiful mountainous hinterland. It's long been famous for its handmade leather goods, available at numerous shops clustered in the town centre.

✚ E6 🍴 Cafés, restaurants, bars ♿ Few 🛈 Calle Morena de Mora 19A, tel 956 46 49 00

VÉJER DE LA FRONTERA

www.turismovejer.com
Véjer is a magical little town, a genuine time-capsule, wrapped within medieval walls high on a craggy hill within sight of the sea. The narrow lanes, whitewashed arches and twisting passages are reminders of five and a half centuries of Islamic rule. Spectacular beaches are just a short drive away.

✚ C8 🍴 Cafés, restaurants, bars ♿ Few 🛈 Avenida Los Remedios 2, tel 956 45 17 36

Flamingos in the Parque Nacional Coto de Doñana

The jumble of streets in Véjer de la Frontera

A Drive Through Sevillian Plains

An easy drive through the La Campiña Sevillano, the Sevillian plains west of the Andalucian capital, taking in some elegant towns.

DISTANCE: 115km (71 miles) **ALLOW:** 8 hours (including stops)

START .... **END**

CARMONA
D3

CARMONA

❶ Begin with a stroll around Carmona (▷ 63), taking in the regal sights of this most graceful of cities. The Alcázar, now a *parador*, is good for coffee on the panoramic terrace.

❷ Travel through the plains along the A4 (E5) to reach Écija, 53km (33 miles) east. As you approach the white town emerges, a memorable sight with its soaring belltowers.

❸ Once within the city walls, explore the whitewashed streets to find the 18th-century Palacio de Benamejí, now an engaging carriage museum.

❹ The Iglesia de San Juan Bautista has a fine belltower. From Écija, head south for 34km (21 miles) along the A351, passing fields of sunflowers, to Osuna (▷ 66).

❽ Pick up some delicious pastries from the local convents. From Marchena, return to the A380 and continue north back to Carmona.

❼ Sections of the original walls survive, but the town is a jumble of historic and modern edifices. The 14th-century Mudéjar church of San Juan Bautista includes an excellent parish museum with a fine collection of paintings by Zurbarán.

❻ Take the A92 motorway west of Osuna, following signs for Sevilla (▷ 56), bearing right just after La Puebla de Cazalla onto the A380. After 15km (9 miles), you'll reach modest Marchena.

❺ From a distance, Osuna looks unappealing, but the centre is a gem.

68

A Drive in the Mountains

This drive plunges into the mountains behind Málaga, tracing a route through some of the prettiest *pueblos blancos*.

DISTANCE: 200km (124 miles)   **ALLOW:** 12 hours (including stops)

START

MÁLAGA
🚌 H6

1 Leave Málaga (▷ 24) on the A-357, heading west. After 53km (33 miles), you will come to two roundabouts next to the reservoir El Conde de Guadalhorce.

2 Take the second exit at the first roundabout and the first exit at the second, following signs for the A-367 and continue on this road for 41km (25 miles) to Ronda (▷ 54–55).

3 Explore the city and enjoy the fine views. Leave Ronda on the A-374, following signs for Algodonales, and more wonderful views of the rolling sierras.

4 Take the first turning to the left onto the A-372, heading toward Grazalema. This area is the protected Natural Park of the Sierra de Grazalema, famous for its cork oaks.

END

ARCOS DE LA FRONTERA
🚌 D6

8 Leave the town the same way that you arrived, along the A-373, but turn left onto the A-372 to reach the dramatic Arcos de la Frontera (▷ 63).

7 Leaving Grazalema, continue on the A-372 and, before reaching El Bosque, bear left onto the A-373 and continue to Ubrique (▷ 67). Stop and stretch your legs, and consider purchasing some of the famous handmade leather goods, all made locally.

6 Stay on the A-372 and you arrive at the village of Grazalema (▷ 66). Stop for lunch and have a stroll around the picture-postcard white village, nestling beneath a massive crag.

5 This area is also famous for being the wettest region of Spain.

Shopping

ARTESANÍA ESPAÑOLA

A wonderful crafts shop with a particularly good range of local ceramics; this is a great place to come to find traditional souvenirs and great gifts. Many of the patterns are inspired by ancient Moorish designs.

➕ G7 ✉ Calle Caridad 2, Marbella ☎ 952 82 34 96

BERSHKA

www.bershka.com

A branch of a hugely popular Spanish chain geared toward young women, with very low prices. The accessories are fun and colourful, and there's a great selection of summer beachwear and flip-flops.

➕ B7 ✉ Avenida de las Cortes s/n, Cadiz ☎ 956 26 13 78

CERÁMICA SANTA ANA

A townhouse with a colourfully decorated façade encrusted with tiles, this shop has an enormous range of typical Andalucian ceramics. You can buy figurines, vases, bowls, platters and, of course, the prettily painted tiles.

➕ C3 ✉ Calle San Jorge 31, Sevilla ☎ 954 33 39 90

COLORE CALORE, TARIFA

This small shop on a corner of Tarifa's main street, just next to the port, sells everything in the way of souvenirs and beach equipment. You'll find flip-flops, maps and postcards, ceramics and beach towels.

➕ D9 ✉ Calle Sancho IV 38, Tarifa ☎ 956 68 08 97

DÉJÀ VUE

www.dejavumarbella.com

A tiny little boutique with vintage fashion for men and women. Also a quirky collection of books, decorative items and furniture. If you are looking for an antique beaded dress from the 1920s or some retro-chic sunglasses from the 1980s, come here.

➕ G7 ✉ Calle Pedraza 8, Marbella ☎ 952 82 55 21

ENRILE

This exclusive shop has a fine selection of exquisitely handcrafted leather goods, leather saddles and riding gear, plus belts, shoes and jackets.

➕ C3 ✉ Calle Montecarmelo 63D, Sevilla ☎ 954 27 45 90

UBRIQUE'S LEATHER

Ubrique (▷ 67), a white village spectacularly located next to a huge ravine in the Sierra of Grazalema, is famous throughout Spain for its high quality leather goods. Amble along the main street, Avenida San Pascual, to find numerous boutiques selling an enormous selection of locally made shoes, bags, clothing and belts.

IBÉRICOS DE MONTANERA

The hills north of Córdoba are famous for their succulent cured ham and charcuterie. This delicatessen has a fine selection of some of the best and most sought-after *jamón Pata Negra* (made with free range pigs reared on acorns). It can be vacuum-packed if you want to bring some home.

➕ G1 ✉ Plaza de las Tendillas 2, Córdoba ☎ 957 48 84 90

IDEAS DEL MUNDO

Clothing made with natural wool and cotton, leather accessories, South American coffees and chocolates are just some of the Fair Trade products available in this shop. The knowledgeable staff can explain where each item comes from and how it was made.

➕ G1 ✉ Calle Claudio Marcelo 1, Córdoba ☎ 957 47 48 80

JIMMY CHOO

One of just three Spanish boutiques dedicated to the celebrated shoe designer, Jimmy Choo, can be found in Puerto Banús. All the latest designs are here, from jewelled sandals to teetering stilettos and sleek winter boots. Fashionistas will also drool over the fabulous accessories, including sunglasses and bags—choose one of the

shiny patent satchel bags, or the luxurious slouchy Ella bag.
➕ F7 ✉ Casa 'N', Mulle Ribera, Puerto Banús ☎ 952 90 80 43

KONTIKI
www.kontiki.biz
A relaxed, boho-chic boutique, Kontiki sells handmade products imported from Asia, America and Africa. It specializes in silver, precious stones, clothes and accessories.
➕ C6 ✉ Calle Honda 15, Jerez de la Frontera ☎ 956 32 40 24

LOEWE
www.loewe.es
Loewe is the most famous Spanish luxury brand, and has sleek designer fashions for men and women, shoes, accessories and fragrances.
➕ F7 ✉ Calle Ricardo Soriano, Puerto Banús ☎ 952 81 62 65

MARKETS
Mijas hosts some of the best and most colourful street markets on the Costa. You'll find ceramics, handicrafts, shoes, fresh vegetables or flowers, and an authentic atmosphere punctuated by the hoarse cries of stallholders. The markets are held in the mornings, from 9am–2pm.
➕ H6 ✉ Wed market in La Cala, Mijas Costa. Sat market on Camino Viejo de Coín, Las Lagunas, Mijas Costa

MIS ANGELES
www.franquiciamisangeles.com
A curious shop, with all kinds of quirky and original objects relating to the world of angels. Good for unusual souvenirs.
➕ C3 ✉ Calle Rosario 8, Local 6, Sevilla ☎ 954 21 83 65

MUÑOZ SOTO
Come for a rummage around this celebrated antique shop, with an array of crafts, antiques, drawings of local scenes and a variety of souvenirs.
➕ F6 ✉ Calle San Juan de Dios de Córdoba 34, Ronda ☎ 952 87 14 51

EL NIÑO
www.elnino-sweetwear.es
Tarifa, with its glorious windswept beaches, is a mecca for surfers. Get the surfer look at this boutique, which sells its own-design clothing as well as more established labels.

THE GOLDEN MILE
Puerto Banús is the most exclusive resort in Andalucia and it attracts countless celebrities, royalty and famous sports stars. Take a stroll along the 'golden mile' for some seriously upmarket window-shopping: all the big, international designers can be found in the vicinity, including Valentino, Missoni, Fendi, Salvatore Ferragamo, Bulgari, Lanvin and Bottega Venetta.

➕ D9 ✉ Calle Batalla del Salado 39A, Tarifa ☎ 956 68 45 93

NOBUK
Just off Estepona's main shopping street, you'll find this small boutique selling high quality leather accessories, such as wallets, bags and belts.
➕ F7 ✉ Calle Viento 18-20, Estepona ☎ 952 80 01 78

OCTOPUS
www.octopusjerez.com
If you're looking for something different, try Octopus. It sells urban clothing from Spanish designers, as well as original handmade shoes and ethnic jewellery.
➕ C6 ✉ Calle Francos, 16, Jerez de la Frontera ☎ 956 34 33 64

PLATAMODA
Córdoba has been associated with the silver trade since Europeans discovered the Americas. This boutique has original and stylish silver jewellery at reasonable prices.
➕ G1 ✉ Puerta de Almodóvar 6, Córdoba ☎ 957 29 84 95

TINOCO
One of the oldest stores in the city, this delightfully old-fashioned shop offers courteous service and a range of classic clothing. Very picturesque, it attracts almost as many sightseers as shoppers.
➕ B7 ✉ Calle Compañía 1–3, Cádiz ☎ 956 21 22 62

Entertainment and Activities

ANDALUCIAN ADVENTURE

www.andalucianadventure.com
A British-German couple run this friendly adventure holiday company. They specialize in mountain-biking and hiking trips, but can also arrange hot-air ballooning, rock-climbing, caving and abseiling.
🔲 E5 ⊠ Calle Concepción 104, Algodonales ☎ 956 13 73 91

AUTOMATICO MUZIK BAR

www.myspace.com/automaticomuzikbar
A modern, fashionable bar, which attracts an alternative crowd of independent music-lovers and B-movie addicts.
🔲 G1 ⊠ Calle Alfaros 4, Córdoba ☎ No phone ⏰ Daily 5pm–late

BAMBOO

Decorated like a tropical garden, the saloon of Bamboo is full of sofas and cushions. Enjoy chill-out sounds, as you sip on cocktails.
🔲 D9 ⊠ Plaza de la Alameda 2, Tarifa ☎ No phone ⏰ Daily 9am–3am

BARRA FIJA

This traditional café-bar is a relaxed spot, popular all day and all night with a varying crowd of locals. Come for breakfast, snacks, coffee or a cocktail.
🔲 G1 ⊠ Camino de los Sastres s/n, Córdoba ☎ 957 46 84 08 ⏰ Daily 9am–3am

CAFÉ TEATRO PAY PAY

www.cafeteatropaypay.com
A small theatre-café with a bohemian atmosphere, this is a local classic. It hosts excellent live shows and concerts by up-and-coming artists. Check out the new talent often discovered here.
🔲 B7 ⊠ Calle del Silencio 1, Cádiz ☎ 956 25 25 43 ⏰ Shows start at 10.30pm

CAPOTE

www.terrazacapote.com
This summer *terraza* (an outdoor bar) is situated on the Paseo de Colón, next to the Triana Bridge. Overlooking the breezy River Guadalquivir, it is the ideal place for a drink during Sevilla's hot summer nights.
🔲 C3 ⊠ Bajos del Puente de Triana, Sevilla ☎ 954 56 38 58 ⏰ Daily noon–3am

SUMMER NIGHTS

Sevilla is one of the hottest cities in Spain, and even locals have trouble sleeping during the sweltering summer nights. By day, the city drowses, bludgeoned by temperatures that can reach 40 degrees, but, at night, Sevillanos emerge from their homes to stroll along the banks of the River Guadalquivir. Numerous *terrazas* are clustered here, where you can join the locals to eat, drink and dance until dawn.

LA COMEDIA

One of the oldest clubs in Puerto Banús, this is where all the locals go once the bars have closed.
🔲 F7 ⊠ Plaza de La Comedia, Puerto Banús ☎ 952 77 64 78 ⏰ Daily 11pm–7am

DUENDE COPAS

www.duendecopas.es
Estepona's marina (Puerto Deportivo) has some good bars and clubs. Duende is one of the most reliable clubs around the port, with mainstream pop music and regular theme parties.
🔲 F7 ⊠ Puerto Deportivo 22, Estepona ☎ 667 68 82 41 ⏰ Daily 10pm–4am

FUN BEACH

One of the largest clubs in Europe with numerous dance floors playing different sorts of dance music. A favourite with teenagers earlier on, the crowd gets older as the night wears on.
🔲 H6 ⊠ Avenida Palma de Mallorca 7, Torremolinos ☎ 952 05 23 97 ⏰ Daily 8pm–6am

KAFKA

This modern, designer nightclub has two spaces. There's a mellow chill-out lounge, for chatting with friends without shouting over the music, and a lively dance floor area.
🔲 C3 ⊠ Calle Faustino Álvarez 27, Sevilla ☎ No phone ⏰ Thu–Sat from 11pm–late

MISIANA
www.misiana.com
A hotel, café, restaurant and bar in the centre of Tarifa's old town, this is very cool and beautifully designed. Opt for a perfectly mixed cocktail at the bar, and choose from a range of gourmet tapas.
✚ D9 ✉ Calle Sancho IV El Bravo, Tarifa ☎ 956 62 70 83 🕐 Daily 9am–2am

EL PARAISO GOLF CLUB
www.elparaisogolfclub.com
This championship golf course is one of the oldest in the region, and its greens are among the finest on the Costa del Sol. On the edge of Estepona, it enjoys spectacular sea and mountain views.
✚ F7 ✉ Ctra. de Cádiz km 167, Estepona ☎ 952 88 38 35

EL PERRO ANDALUZ
This mellow bar is filled with mismatched furniture and surreal decoration. It fills up with a bohemian crowd as the night wears on. WiFi is available. There are occasional live gigs, including flamenco on Sunday.
✚ C3 ✉ Calle Bustos Tavera 4, Sevilla ☎ 954 22 20 29 🕐 Daily 11pm–late

PLATO 68
www.plato68.com
Estepona's 'superclub' has Tony Martinez as resident DJ on Fridays and Deejay J Aragon on Saturdays, plus regular guests year round.
✚ F7 ✉ Avenida Juan Carlos I 68, Estepona ☎ 670 50 31 24 🕐 Fri–Sat midnight–7am

RIO REAL GOLF CLUB
www.rioreal.com
There are more than 60 golf courses on the Costa del Sol and this is considered to be one of the most spectacular. Located 3km (2 miles) from Marbella, the 18-hole course is suitable for golfers of every level. Classes are available.
✚ G7 ✉ Urb. Rio Real, Marbella ☎ 952 76 57 33

SALA CAPITOLIUM
Situated in La Punta de San Felipe, the heart of Cádiz's nightlife zone, this is a buzzy music bar, with a dance floor and popular Sunday karaoke sessions.
✚ B7 ✉ Paseo de Pascual Pery, Cádiz ☎ No phone 🕐 Mon–Wed midnight–6am, Thu–Sun 1am–7am

CAMARÓN DE LA ISLA
The birthplace of flamenco is the province of Cádiz, particularly the city of Jerez. El Camarón de la Isla (1950–1992), universally recognized as the greatest 20th-century flamenco artist, was born in nearby San Fernando. There is a signposted route around the city (details at the tourist office ✉ Alameda Cristina, Edificio Los Claustris ☎ 956 34 17 11), which takes all in the main sights associated with the great artist.

TABERNA CASA MADRILES
A traditional tavern, this offers a good range of wines, with a special emphasis on local products. Tapas are still offered free with each drink, according to traditional Andalucian custom. Try the *champanillo* or the pleasant *vino dulce*—surprisingly refreshing when served chilled.
✚ G1 ✉ Camino de los Sastres 30, Córdoba ☎ 678 57 22 10 🕐 Daily 8pm–2am (until 3am at weekends)

LA TABERNA FLAMENCA
www.latabernaflamenca.com
Jerez is considered the cradle of flamenco. Enjoy a live flamenco show and dine on local specialties at this popular *tablao*.
✚ C6 ✉ Calle Angostillo de Santiago 3, Jerez de la Frontera ☎ 956 32 36 93 🕐 Mid-May–end Oct Wed–Thu and Sat 2.30pm and 10.30pm, Mon–Tue and Sun 10.30pm; Nov–mid May Wed and Sat 10.30pm

TARIFA MAX KITESURFING SCHOOL
www.tarifamax.net
Tarifa is world-famous for its surfing, and this establishment offers kitesurfing lessons for beginners, as well as private classes for the more advanced. All the latest in kitesurfing equipment here.
✚ D9 ✉ Ctra. Nac. 340 km 76, Tarifa ☎ 696 55 82 27

Restaurants

PRICES

Prices are approximate, based on a 3-course meal for one person.
€€€   over €45
€€   €25–€45
€   under €25

EL ANGELOTE (€)

This is a charming spot for decent home-cooked fare at a modest price. Try the *porra ante-querana* (a variation on gazpacho) and finish up with *bienmesabe antequerano* with almonds and cinnamon.
🟦 H5 🖂 Plaza Coso Viejo s/n, Antequera ☎ 952 70 34 65 🕓 Lunch and dinner; closed Mon

ARROCERIA LA PEPA (€€€)

www.restaurantelapepa.com
Right on the beachfront, this traditional restaurant has a fabulous terrace for alfresco dining. The Mediterranean rice dishes include several different varieties of paella (which are highly recommended), but you can also choose from a wide range of meat and fish specialties.
🟦 B7 🖂 Paseo Marítimo 14, Cádiz ☎ 956 26 38 21 🕓 Daily lunch and dinner

BAR BRENES (€)

One of the most authentic and popular bars in town, this offers big portions of tapas and *raciones*, as well as the local favourite of fried fish. Join the locals out on the terrace.
🟦 B7 🖂 Calle Medina Sidonia 11, Cádiz ☎ 956 27 47 03 🕓 Daily 8am–midnight

BAR LA GIRALDA (€)

Situated in ancient Arab baths, within sight of the emblematic cathedral, this central bar is famous with locals and tourists alike. The tapas are some of the best in the city and the list is enormous.
🟦 C3 🖂 Calle Mateos Gago 1, Sevilla ☎ 954 22 74 35 🕓 Mon–Sat 9.30am–12.30am

BAR JUANITO (€)

www.bar-juanito.com
Try a wide variety of tapas with a glass of chilled sherry on the magnificent terrace of this bar just off Plaza del Arenal. They also have a shop opposite the bar selling local products.
🟦 F6 🖂 Calle Pescadería Vieja 8-10, Jerez de la Frontera ☎ 956 33 48 38 🕓 Tue–Sun 8pm–1am

RONDA AND ROBO DE TORO

Visit Ronda's Plaza de Toros (bullring and museum), built in 1785, to hear about Pedro Romero, founder of the classical Ronda school of bullfighting and the first matador to fight *a pie* (on foot). Try the popular local dish *rabo de toro* (literally 'bull tail') said to be best immediately after a *corrida* (bullfight).

BODEGA SABOR ANDALUZ (€)

www.bodegasaborandaluz.com
Fine Iberian hams and charcuterie are the specialties here. Try the *jamón de bellota* (▷ panel, 75), served in wafer-thin, almost transparent slices, which melt in the mouth.
🟦 F7 🖂 Calle Claridad 44, Estepona ☎ 952 79 10 30 🕓 Daily lunch and dinner

EL CABALLO ROJO (€€€)

www.elcaballorojo.com
This renowned, family-owned eatery is housed in a typical Córdoba town house and has welcomed Spanish Royalty and illustrious political figures to its tables. The menu offers typical Andalucian dishes and it's famed for its desserts.
🟦 G1 🖂 Cardenal Herrero 28, Córdoba ☎ 957 47 53 75 🕓 Tue–Sat lunch and dinner, Sun lunch

CÁDIZ EL CHICO (€€)

This traditional restaurant, in the heart of the pretty, whitewashed mountain village of Grazalema, serves local dishes that range from seafood to local lamb. In winter, dine in front of a roaring fire.
🟦 E6 🖂 Plaza de España 8, Grazalema ☎ 956 13 20 27 🕓 Daily lunch and dinner

LA CARBONA (€€)

www.lacarbona.com
Located in a beautifully restored former sherry

bodega in a city whose name is synomous with the drink, this charming restaurant serves local cuisine, with a wide range of meat and fish dishes.
✚ C6 ✉ Calle San Francisco de Paula 2, Jerez de la Frontera ☎ 956 34 74 75 🕐 Daily noon–midnight

CASA JUAN (€€€)

This seaside restaurant has been decorated to look like the inside of a ship, and serves some of the best local seafood around. The *pescadito frito* (fried fish) is certainly one of the best choices, but you can also choose from classic Mediterranean rice dishes.
✚ H6 ✉ Calle San Ginés 20, La Carihuela, Torremolinos ☎ 952 37 35 12 🕐 Lunch and dinner; closed Mon

CASA PABLO (€€)

Prettily set on the loveliest square in Estepona's whitewashed old town, this classic restaurant serves traditional Andalucian dishes such as gazpacho and fried fish. Dine on the terrace, overlooking the square.
✚ F7 ✉ Plaza de las Flores 13, Estepona ☎ 952 80 12 99 🕐 Lunch and dinner; closed Wed

CERVECERIA EL TONELITO (€)

A resolutely old-fashioned tapas bar, with a huge range of dishes on offer. Try the *croquetas* and the delicious Iberian hams.

✚ G7 ✉ Calle Pantaleón 4, Marbella ☎ 952 86 74 06 🕐 Mon–Sat dinner

EL CHOCO (€€€)

www.restaurantechoco.com
Kisko García is one of the most talked-about young chefs in Andalucía, celebrated for his refined and original contemporary cuisine. Try the sublime reinvention of the classic Córdoban soup, *salmorejo*, made here with anchovies and cherries.
✚ G1 ✉ Calle Compositor Serrano Lucena 14, Córdoba ☎ 957 26 48 63 🕐 Lunch and dinner; closed Sun dinner and Mon

EL CHOTO (€)

Located in the enchanting labyrinth of Córdoba's Jewish Quarter (La Judería), this authentic restaurant is a classic place to try the traditional local dish of stewed kid (*choto*), accompanied by a robust Córdoban red.

JAMÓN IBÉRICO

The best Spanish ham comes from the free-range, black-footed pigs, who roam the forest and eat a diet comprised largely of acorns (*bellotas*). The finest Andalucian hams are produced in Jabugo, in Huelva province, but are available across the region. The best, and most expensive, is called *jamón Ibérico de bellota,* which is cured for 36 months.

✚ G1 ✉ Calle Almanzor 10, Córdoba ☎ 957 76 01 15 🕐 Lunch and dinner; closed Sun

EL CHURRASCO (€€)

www.elchurrasco.com
Open since 1970, this restaurant's specialty is local cuisine, with a range of meat and fish on the menu as well. The dining room is beautifully decorated but try to get a table on the magnificent colonnaded patio, with its cooling fountain.
✚ G1 ✉ Calle Romero 16, Córdoba ☎ 957 29 08 19 🕐 Mon–Sat lunch and dinner

CREPERIE SANTA FÉ (€)

A delightful French-owned restaurant, serving authentic crêpes with a variety of fillings, both sweet and savoury. They also offer other dishes, including meat and fish, accompanied by an extensive wine list.
✚ D9 ✉ Calle Alameda 9, Tarifa ☎ 956 68 53 62 🕐 Daily dinner

EL DORADO (€)

At El Dorado, Mexican and Columbian cuisine are the highlights on the eclectic menu. House specialties include delicious pasties, *empanadas vallecaucanas*. It's popular with young people thanks to the low prices and friendly service.
✚ B7 ✉ Calle Abreu 9, Cádiz ☎ 956 22 37 45 🕐 Daily lunch and dinner

FREIDURIA LAS FLORES (€)

Cádiz is famous for its fried fish, and Las Flores is one of the most traditional places to try it. Order the *surtido* to get a selection of various fresh fish, which you can choose to eat wrapped in a paper cone, or in the dining room.

➕ B7 ✉ Plaza Topete 4, Cádiz ☎ 956 22 61 12 🕐 Daily 9am–4pm, 8pm–midnight

EL GALLO (€)

A great budget option, this serves simple Andalucian home-cooking, with the emphasis on fresh fish. It also offers an excellent set-price lunch on weekdays.

➕ G7 ✉ Calle Lobatos 44, Marbella ☎ 952 82 79 98 🕐 Lunch and dinner; closed Thu

EL GALLO AZUL (€€)

Probably the most famous tapas bar in town, this has won numerous awards for its varied selection of traditional as well as more elaborate and original gourmet treats.

➕ C6 ✉ Calle Larga 2, Jerez de la Frontera ☎ 956 32 61 48 🕐 Mon–Sat dinner

LA MANDRAGORA (€€€)

www.mandragoratarifa.com This quiet and intimate restaurant, in the old town, serves an exotic fusion of Andalucian-Arabic food. The specialty

is lamb with plums and almonds.

➕ D9 ✉ Calle Independencia 3, Tarifa ☎ 956 68 12 91 🕐 Dinner; closed Sun and two weeks in Feb

LOS MELLI (€)

This friendly tapas bar in Tarifa's old town is famous because it is run by identical twins. Get here early to find a seat—the bar gets packed from 9pm onwards and it's popular with locals. There's also a terrace.

➕ D9 ✉ Calle Guzman El Bueno 16, Tarifa ☎ No phone 🕐 Daily dinner

MERCHÁN 1955 (€€)

An intimate, pretty little restaurant, Merchán 95 has a fine reputation for excellent local specialties, particularly the *fritura de pescado*, prepared with the finest quality olive oil and beautifully fresh fish.

CLASSIC TAPAS

Classic Andalucian tapas include *croquetas*, usually made with ham, but occasionally with cod (*bacalao*), chicken (*pollo*) or spinach (*espinacas*). Several varieties of *tortilla*, thick Spanish omelette, will be on offer, but the best is the local *tortilla de camarones*, made with tiny shrimp. Spicy chorizo is popular, as is all kinds of delicious seafood, from mussels to prawns.

➕ G7 ✉ Calle San Gabriel 10, Marbella ☎ 952 78 01 34 🕐 Lunch and dinner; closed Mon

MESÓN JUDERIA (€€)

A cosy dining room on the first floor of a classic hotel, this serves traditional Andalucian favourites prepared with the best local products.

➕ C8 ✉ Calle Arco de las Monjas, Véjer de la Frontera ☎ 956 44 76 57 🕐 Daily lunch and dinner

PEDRO ROMERO (€€)

www.rpedroromero.com A classic in Ronda, this traditional restaurant is located opposite the bullring, and is named after Pedro Romero (1754–1839), a famous local *torero* (bullfighter), who was still fighting bulls at the age of 80. It's probably the best place to try the local specialty *rabo de toro* (oxtail stew).

➕ F6 ✉ Calle Virgen de la Paz 18, Ronda ☎ 952 87 11 10 🕐 Lunch and dinner; closed Mon

PICASSO (€€)

www.pizzeriapicasso.com With its enviable location overlooking the yacht-filled marina in Puerto Banús, it's no surprise that this restaurant is prime celebrity-spotting territory. Try fresh, modern Italian cuisine, and finish up with the delicious tiramisú.

➕ F7 ✉ Muelle Ribera local 48–49 H, Puerto Banús

☎ 952 81 36 69 ⏰ Daily noon–1am

PIZZERIA DIEGO (€)
www.pizzeriadiego.com
For something quick, cheap and tasty, try the Diego. The pizzas are good, but they also serve simple meat and fish dishes too.
➕ F6 ✉ Calle Virgen del Carmen, local D1, Ronda ☎ 952 87 98 99 ⏰ Daily lunch and dinner

PORTOFINO (€€)
This is a very popular place for a meal on the seafront, but it's best avoided at weekends when it gets overcrowded. Consistently good paella, salads and seafood.
➕ H7 ✉ Paseo Marítimo Rey de España 29, Fuengirola ☎ 952 47 06 43 ⏰ Lunch and dinner; closed Mon and Fri lunch

RESTAURANTE SAN FERNANDO (€€)
Located in a beautifully restored 17th-century townhouse, this serves innovative cooking based on traditional Andalucian recipes. Go for the special tasting menu, which highlights all the specialties. Fabulous desserts.
➕ D3 ✉ Calle Sacramento 3, Carmona ☎ 954 14 35 56 ⏰ Lunch and dinner; closed Sun dinner, Mon and Aug

SOUK (€€)
Be transported to Morocco at Souk, where the low tables and colourful lamps create an intimate and romantic atmosphere. Mint tea and pastries during the afternoons, and cous cous and tagines in the evening. It also serves Thai and Indian dishes, in particular, good curries. Try the tasty *mango creme* for dessert.
➕ D9 ✉ Calle Mar Tireno 11, Tarifa ☎ 956 62 70 65 ⏰ Daily 11am–11pm

TABERNA SAN MIGUEL (€€)
Old photographs and prints of Córdoba, famous bullfighters and local personalities adorn the walls of this charming tavern. Try local dishes such as baby broad beans sautéed with ham and topped with scrambled egg.
➕ G1 ✉ Plaza de San Miguel 1, Córdoba ☎ 957 47 01 66 ⏰ Lunch and dinner; closed Sun

---

PERFECT PAELLA

Paella, the most famous Spanish dish, originated in Valencia, where the plump *bomba* rice, perfect for sucking up the juices, is grown. A good paella should be succulent and juicy, with a light crunchy crust (called the *succarat*), and a delicate golden colour from the saffron (avoid the cafés with pictures of a bright yellow paella–this comes from a packet!).

TANGO (€€)
www.restaurantetango.com
The succulent steaks at this wood-beamed Argentinean restaurant are prepared in myriad ways, and are perfectly matched by the robust house red. Booking is essential in high season and at weekends.
➕ F7 ✉ Avda. Julio Iglesias Edif. Miramar, Puerto Banús ☎ 952 81 23 58 ⏰ Daily dinner

LA TORRECILLA (€€)
A rustically decorated, Andalucian tavern in the delightfully old-fashioned neighbourhood of Triana, this offers a wide range of fresh seafood and shellfish. Wonderful terrace.
➕ C3 ✉ Avenida de Coria 5, Sevilla ☎ 954 34 39 30 ⏰ Mon–Sat 10am–1am

TRAGABUCHES (€€€)
www.tragabuches.com
Outstanding contemporary cuisine prepared by dynamic young chefs, Benito Gómez and Víctor Taborda, is accompanied by an excellent wine list. An unforgettable meal is guaranteed. The *carpaccio* of prawns—a dish traditionally made of beef but interpreted to use wafer thin prawns—is one of their signature dishes. They also run a gourmet tapas bar, Tragatapas, on Calle Nueva.
➕ F6 ✉ Calle José Aparicio 1, Ronda ☎ 952 19 02 91 ⏰ Lunch and dinner; closed Sun dinner and Mon

Granada, capital of the last Moslem kingdom in Spain, is crowned by the Alhambra, a breathtaking palace. Beyond the city, the secluded coves of the Costa Tropical (the Granada coastline), mountainous interior, and isolated villages of the Axarquía are a treat for more active travellers.

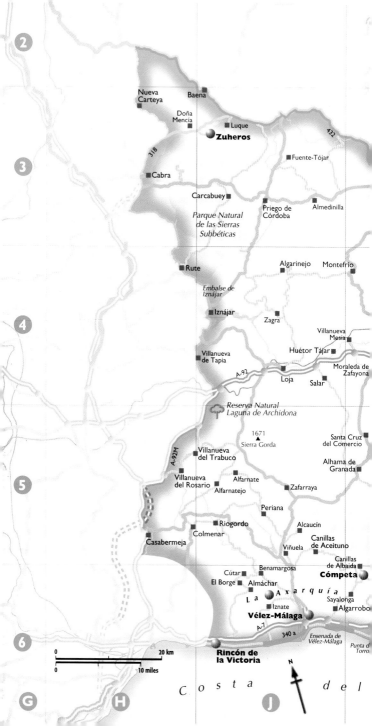

Nueva
Carteya

Baena

Doña
Mencia

Luque

Zuheros

Fuente-Tójar

432

Cabra

318

Carcabuey

*Parque Natural
de las Sierras
Subbéticas*

Priego de
Córdoba

Almedinilla

Rute

Algarinejo

Montefrío

*Embalse de
Iznájar*

Iznájar

Zagra

Villanueva
Mesía

Huétor Tájar

Moraleda de
Zafayona

Villanueva
de Tapia

A-92

Loja

Salar

*Reserva Natural
Laguna de Archidona*

1671
▲
Sierra Gorda

Santa Cruz
del Comercio

Alhama de
Granada

A-92M

Villanueva
del Trabuco

Villanueva
del Rosario

Alfarnate

Alfarnatejo

Zafarraya

Periana

Alcaucín

Riogordo

Colmenar

Viñuela

Canillas
de Aceituno

Casabermeja

Cútar

Benamargosa

Canillas
de Albaida

Cómpeta

El Borge

Almáchar

L a   A x a r q u í a

Iznate

Sayalonga

Algarrobo

Vélez-Málaga

A-7

340 a

*Ensenada de
Vélez-Málaga*

Punta d
Torro

**Rincón de
la Victoria**

0   20 km

0   10 miles

C   o   s   t   a   *d   e   l*

N

Alcalá
la Real

1604
▲
rapanda

Moclín

Íllora

Pinos
Puente

**Casa Museo
Federico
García Lorca**

Fuente
Vaqueros

Maracena

Láchar

Santa
Fé

GRANADA
Albaicín,
Alhambra,
Catedral & Capilla Real,
Monasterio de la Cartuja,
Museo Arqueológico y
Etnológico de Granada
Parque de las Ciencias,
Plaza Bib-Rambla,

Huétor
Vega

Gabia
Grande

Chimeneas

Ogíjares

La Malahá

Alhendín

Otura

Ventas de
Huelma

Dílar

Cacín

Escúzar

Padul

Agrón

Dúrcal

*Embalse de los
Bermejales*

A-44

Lecrín

Arenas
del Rey

Jayena

Albuñuelas

*Parque Natural
Sierras de Tejada,
Almijara y Alhama*

*Embalse de
Béznar*

Sierra

de

1832
▲
Navachica

Almijara

Guájar
Faraguit

Otívar

Itrabo

Frigiliana

Jete

Molvízar

orrox

Salobreña

Nerja

La Herradura

*Punta de
la Mona*

Almuñécar

S o l

Costa Tropical

K

L

Frigiliana

Whitewashed houses cling to the hillside (left); handicrafts for sale in Frigiliana (right)

THE BASICS

www.frigiliana.es

🞧 K6

🍴 Cafés and restaurants

🚌 Several buses a day from Nerja (less frequent in winter months)

🚻 Few

❓ www.viva-malaga.com/frigiliana-tours for personally guided tours of the town

🛈 Cuesta del Apero 10, tel 952 53 42 61; Apr–end Oct Mon–Fri 9.30–7.30, Sat 9.30–2, 4–8, Sun 10–2, 4–8; Nov–end Mar Mon–Fri 9–6, Sat–Sun 10–6

HIGHLIGHT

● Festival Frigiliana *'tres culturas'*: the annual festival of music and dance in August is one of the region's most colourful fiestas. Wine flows freely, folk musicians perform alongside famous Spanish pop groups, and BBQs fill the air with irresistible scents

Heavily laden donkeys and black-clad widows remain a familiar sight in Frigiliana, a picturesque tumble of whitewashed houses magically set against a mountainous backdrop. But as boutique accommodation and art galleries proliferate, it has become an increasingly fashionable retreat.

Casco Histórico Frigiliana's Arabic heritage is evident in the sinuous passages of the Casco Histórico, the redolent old quarter. One of the last battles between the Moors and the Christians was fought here in 1569, and the event is still celebrated every June with an annual pilgrimage honouring the town's patron saint. The narrow lanes are cobbled in intricate Mudéjar patterns, and the immaculate villas are trimmed with window boxes bright with scarlet geraniums. The heart-stopping views over the undulating Sierra Tejeda lend it a poetic romance, and have earned the town several awards for conservation and beauty. Busy in July and August, out of high season you'll find it blissfully peaceful but with enough to keep you entertained.

History and magic History, ghost and magic tours are run throughout the summer from outside the tourist office. While ambling around the town, look out for the painted tiles, which vividly depict stories from Frigiliana's history. It's worth stopping to admire the church of San Antonio and the 17th-century artworks within, and the old granary near the entrance to the town, now a store selling local handicrafts.

Water fountain in the Plaza Nueva (left); the Convento de San Jeronimo (right)

TOP 25

Granada

Capital of the last great Islamic kingdom in Spain, Granada sensuously evokes the lost world of Al-Andalus. Spectacularly set in the foothills of the mighty Sierra Nevada, it is crowned by the Alhambra, one of the greatest Arabic palaces ever built. The modern part of Granada is, however, lively and cosmopolitan.

Unforgettable sights The magical Alhambra (▷ 86–87) is deservedly the most important sight in the city, but Granada has plenty more to offer. The verdant oasis of El Generalife, with its shady avenues and water gardens, is a welcome antidote to the crowds in the Alhambra. Don't miss the Capilla Real, where Ferdinand and Isabella (known as the Catholic Kings) once received Columbus, and where they chose to be buried.

Exotic neighbourhoods Much of the city's charm lies in exploring its Moorish heart, particularly the whitewashed maze of the Albaicín quarter (▷ 84–85), and the *gitano* (gypsy) cave district of Sacromonte. Here, the mournful strains of flamenco can be heard day and night, and impromptu performances often break out in the plazas. For a truly memorable experience check into one of the many cave apartments (▷ panel, 111), which give wonderful views of the Alhambra and surrounding countryside. It is important to be wary of wandering around alone at night, and note that that getting into one of the local *peñas*—flamenco bars—is tough unless you go with a local.

THE BASICS

www.turismodegranada.org
(provincial tourist information)
www.granadatur.com
(municipal tourist information)
➕ L4
🍴 Numerous cafés, bars and restaurants
♿ Good
ℹ Regional tourist office, Plaza de Mariana Pineda, tel 958 24 71 46. Municipal tourist office, Calle Virgen Blanca 9, tel 902 40 50 45

HIGHLIGHTS

● The Alhambra palace
● Capilla Real
● Albaicín quarter
● Cave apartments

Granada: Albaicín

- Catching sunset over the Alhambra from one of the Carmen cafés
- The Patio de los Naranjas (orange courtyard), Iglesia de Santa Ana
- Moroccan influence

TIPS

- Look out for the Albaicín's distinctive 'Hand of Fatima' door-knockers, warding off the evil eye.
- Soak away your sins at the Hammam Baños Arabes.

There's magic in the air in Spain's most beautifully preserved Arabic quarter, the Albaicín. Forget the map and get lost in this steep _barrio_ of whitewashed villas where secret gardens evoke the seductive perfume of jasmine and orange blossom.

Mosques and churches Albaicín, piled steeply on a hillside facing the Alhambra, means 'people of Baeza', and acquired its name in 1227 when Baeza's Moslems fled here after their city was razed. It was once home to a substantial Moslem community, who constructed more than 30 mosques. Most were demolished after the Reconquest, their stones reused in the construction of churches. The most important Mosque was replaced by the Iglesia de San Salvador, on the Plaza de San Salvador. Recently, the area has

Houses in the Albaicín, the old Arabic quarter of Granada (left); impressive view down to the Albaicín (right)

once again revived its historic tradition of religious tolerance, and is presided over by the gleaming Mezquita de Granada. This opened in 2003, and was the first mosque to be built in Granada since the fall of the city in 1492. Nearby is the Iglesia de Santa Ana, built in 1537, and overlooked by an intricate Mudéjar tower. Few other vestiges of the Moorish heritage survive, although you can still admire the mighty city gates: Elvira, Monaita, de las Pesas, and the graceful remnants of Bab-Al-Bonud.

Little Morocco The southern reaches of the Albaicín, nearest the Plaza Nueva, retain a souk-like atmosphere, and indeed this area formed part of the medina before the Christian Reconquest. It is now famous for its *teterías* (Arabic tea houses) and shops selling Moroccan handicrafts and leather slippers.

THE BASICS

➕ L4
🍴 Several cafés and restaurants
🚌 Buses 31 and 32 from the Plaza Nueva
♿ Few
ℹ️ Plaza de Mariana Pineda, tel 958 24 71 46

Granada: Alhambra

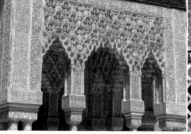

HIGHLIGHTS

- Night Tours
- The Patio de los Leones
- The tranquil Generalife
- The Nasrid palaces
- Spectacular views

TIP

- Try reading a copy of Washington Irving's *Tales of the Alhambra*; Salman Rushdie's *The Moor's Last Sigh*; Phillipa Gregory's *The Constant Princess*; and Paulo Coelho's *The Alchemist.*

'A pearl set in emeralds' sang the Moorish poets of their great palace, the Alhambra. A sublime construction of intricate beauty, it stands as moving testament to the great Nasrid dynasty, rulers of the powerful Kingdom of Granada.

Art and architecture The Alhambra properly refers to a large, walled complex built atop the loftiest hill in Granada, where the sultan and the court of the Kingdom of Granada resided. At the heart of the complex are the mesmerizing Nasrid palaces. At the eastern end are the remnants of the military fortress, which offers breathtaking views of the Albaicín and the snow-clad peaks of the Sierra Nevada. The main mosque, converted into a church after the Reconquest, is still topped with a minaret masquerading as a belltower.

Clockwise from top left: peace and tranquillity in the gardens of Granada's Alhambra; the Plaza de los Aljibes beside the towers of the Alcazaba in the Alhambra; looking through the arch of Palacios Nazaries to the city; stunning mosaic tiles at the Patio de los Arrayanes; intricate carvings can be seen at the Patio de los Leones

After the fall of Granada, subsequent monarchs substantially modified parts of the Alhambra: the Palacio de Carlos V (Carlos I of Spain) is an ornate, Renaissance construction, which contains a museum dedicated to the Alhambra's history. The Generalife, a sumptuous Nasrid summer palace surrounded by perfumed gardens, remains a soothing oasis of tinkling fountains and lush vegetation.

The Nasrid palaces The most magical section of the Alhambra, the Nasrid palaces are constructed with a poetic precision and delicacy. Columns are ethereally slender; stucco ceilings appear to have been spun from icing sugar and the soothing sounds are everywhere. Many of the courtyards, most notably the celebrated Patio de los Leones, are arranged around limpid pools, which perfectly reflect the full moon.

THE BASICS

www.alhambra-patronato.es

🔒 L4

✉ Calle Real s/n

☎ 958 02 79 00

🕐 Mar–end Oct daily 8.30–8 (also Fri–Sat 10pm–11.30pm); Nov–end Feb daily 8.30–6 (also Fri–Sat 8pm–9.30pm)

🍴 Snack kiosk; restaurant

🚌 Alhambra minibus 30 and 32 from the Plaza Nueva

♿ Few

💰 Expensive. Pre-booking advised; try to visit off season

Hiking in La Axarquía

TOP 25

This rugged region, dotted with white-washed villages, remains a refreshingly isolated retreat from the mayhem on the coast. Terraced orchards, first established by the Arabs, still line the hillsides.

Tropical gardens Walking here offers something for everyone, from casual ramblers to more serious trekkers. To the south the terraced slopes are planted with date palms and avocados, *chirimoya* (custard apple) and mangos, olives and lemon trees. Come in spring, when the trees are awash with blossom. There are numerous trails linking the largely undiscovered villages—these can be joined for substantial treks over several days, or you can pick a base and enjoy one of the day walks. The trails vary in length from one to nine hours. To the north, the terrain becomes

The attractive town of Vélez-Málaga lies at the foot of the Axarquía mountains (left);
Torrox, a pretty town within the Axarquía region, makes a great base for a walking
holiday (right)

increasingly rugged, culminating in the forbidding
granite peaks of the Puerto Blanquillo, beyond
which lie the Granada plains.

Days of wine and sausages Cómpeta (▷ 93)
is perhaps the most spectacular of the villages in
the area, but each offers a unique charm. This is
largely derived from the singular traditions, which
which are preserved in annual—sometimes eccentric—festivals. During Cómpeta's wine festival, held
every August, the town's fountains run with Jarel,
the delicious sweet local wine. On the Sunday
before Christmas, Torrox celebrates the *Fiesta de
las Migas*, a classic peasant dish of breadcrumbs
cooked up with vegetables and meat. In Canillas
de Aceituno, the *Día de la Morcilla* (Day of the
Blood Pudding) fiesta, held in April, celebrates the
bounty of November's *matanza* (pig slaughter).

THE BASICS

🔀 J6

🍽 Numerous restaurants
and cafés. Try Venta de
Alfarnate (▷ 106)

🚌 Buses from Málaga and
Nerja serve most villages in
the region, but a car is best

🚹 Few

❓ Useful websites include
www.absoluteaxarquia.com
and www.la-axarquia.com

Nerja

The town of Nerja has lots to offer with its spectacular setting and interesting caves

THE BASICS

www.nerja.org

🔂 K6

🍴 Numerous cafés, bars and restaurants. Try the chorizo infierno at Los Barriles (▷ 103)

🚌 Hourly bus connections to Málaga and seven buses daily to Granada

♿ Few (none at the Cueva del Nerja)

🎉 *Carnaval* (Feb/Mar), *Semana Santa* (Easter), *San Isidro* (15 May), *Fiesta de la Virgen del Carmen* (16 Jul), *Feria de Nerja* (2nd week Oct)

ℹ️ Calle Carmen 1, tel 952 52 15 31

HIGHLIGHTS

● Ice cream in the moonlight on the Balcón de Europa
● Cueva de Nerja
● Tropical beaches

The prettiest town on the eastern Costa del Sol, the former fishing village of Nerja is now a cosmopolitan resort. The old town retains its traditional charm, but visitors will also find day spas, fine restaurants and a lively party scene.

The old quarter The lovingly restored old town of Nerja is perfect for an aimless stroll. Explore the cobblestoned streets, many of which have been pedestrianized and are lined with immaculately whitewashed villas, each trimmed with flower-filled balconies. Visitors and locals alike congregate day and night on the world-famous Balcón de Europa, a spectacular promenade offering a breathtaking panorama out over the Mediterranean.

Cueva de Nerja The town's most famous attraction is the Cueva de Nerja, accidentally discovered by some local boys in the 1950s. These fairy-tale grottoes, with their pale accretions in fantastical forms, have become one of Spain's top attractions. You might want to plan your visit to coincide with the annual International Festival of Music and Dance, which takes place here in July.

Tropical beaches Nerja is blessed with glorious beaches. These sandy coves, backed by lush gardens and terracotta-hued cliffs, are accessed by steep steps. The most dramatic descents are found to the east (Burriana) and west (Torrecillo). A walkway from the Paseo de los Caribineros skirts several coves before arriving at the popular Playa de Burriana.

Zuheros

A rural idyll—the pretty village of Zuheros (left); ruined fortress hewn from the cliff (right)

Tucked away in the hinterland between Granada and Jaén, this pretty white village hangs between the peaks of the Sierra Subbética, fringed by groves of almond and olive trees. Long overlooked, the village has recently been discovered by artists and writers, as well as walkers following the Via Verde.

Uncharted territory It's thought that Zuheros was founded in the 9th century, when it formed part of the kingdom of Granada. A small fortress was hewn from the rock to guard the kingdom's northern frontier, which was later rebuilt and extended after the Reconquest. The remnants of the castle still dominate the village, and it's well worth the scramble up to the ruins to enjoy panoramic views over the surrounding mountains. As in so many Andalucian villages, the Mezquita was transformed into a church, the Iglesia de los Remedios, and its minaret now does service as a belltower. Still a sleepy, agricultural community involved in the production of olives, Zuheros has also benefited from the growth of rural tourism.

Cueva de los Murciélagos The 'Cave of Bats' is situated on the fringes of the village, and has contributed to Zuheros' growing popularity with visitors. There are some 60 caves in total, forming a complicated network of which just a short section is open for visits. As well as the natural beauty of the stalactites and stalagmites, this is one of the most important Neolithic sites on the Iberian peninsula adorned with impressive paintings.

More to See

ALMUÑÉCAR

www.almunecar.info

Almuñécar is undistinguishable from other Costa resorts along its sea-front, but step into the old town of Sexitano and you'll discover a world of atmospheric tapas bars and the only authentic flamenco *peña* (folk club) on the coast (▷ 102). Kids will enjoy the Ornithological Park filled with tropical plants and brightly col-oured parrots. If jazz is your thing the International Jazz Festival in July is a good time to visit.

✚ L6   🍽 Numerous cafes, restaurants, bars   🚌 Regular buses from Granada, local buses from Nerja   🚻 Few   🦜 Ornithological Park moderate   🛈 Palacete de la Najarra, Avda de Europa s/n, tel 958 63 11 25

CÓMPETA

www.competa.es

Beautifully set amid rolling hills, Cómpeta is one of the loveliest vil-lages of La Axarquía (▷ 88–89). An important silk-producing town during Arab times, its Moorish heritage is still evident in the twisting maze of narrow lanes and low, whitewashed houses. Numerous walks splinter off into the surrounding hills, where olive groves and vines grow in intricate terraces.

✚ K6   🕐 Summer Tue–Fri 9–2, 3–8, Sat 10–3; winter Wed–Sat 9–2, 3–6, Sun 10–3   🍽 Limited cafés, restaurants, bars   🚌 Infrequent bus service from Málaga   🚻 Few   🛈 Avda de Constitución s/n, tel 952 55 36 85

FUENTE VAQUEROS: CASA MUSEO FEDERICO GARCÍA LORCA

www.museogarcialorca.org

The birthplace of Andalucía's most celebrated poet and dramatist Federico García Lorca (1898–1936) has been converted into an intimate museum, faithfully restored to its orig-inal appearance, and full of personal mementoes. Lorca's most famous trilogy (*Blood Wedding*, *Yerma* and *The House of Bernada Alba*) are pas-sionate and deeply moving portrayals of life in rural Andalucía. In 1936, Lorca was shot by Nationalists and thrown into an unmarked grave near

The waterfront resort of Almuñécar

The attractive hillside town of Cómpeta

Víznar. His remains have never been found, but a park has been laid out in his memory.

K4 ⊠ Calle Poeta García Lorca 4, Fuente Vaqueros (17km/11 miles west of Granada) ☎ 958 51 64 53 ⏰ Tue–Sun 10am–1pm, 4pm–8pm ❚❚ Limited cafés and restaurants in Fuente Vaqueros ♿ Few ❓ Granada's tourist office offers a one-day tour of the main Lorca sights in the region

GRANADA: CATEDRAL AND CAPILLA REAL

Granada's cathedral stands testament to the determination of the Catholic Kings who conquered the last Moslem kingdom of Spain. Construction began in 1521, and work was directed by Diego de Siloé from 1528–1563. The original Gothic edifice with a beautiful Renaissance dome was substantially remodelled in the 18th century, when the baroque ornamentation was added. The sumptuously decorated Capilla Real, where Ferdinand and Isabella are buried in lavishly carved marble tombs, has a separate entrance (on Calle Oficios).

L4 ⊠ Gran Vía de Colón 5 ☎ 958 22 29 59 ⏰ Apr–end Oct Mon–Sat 10.45–1.30, 4–8, Sun and public hols 4–8; Nov–end Mar Mon–Sat 10.45–1.30, 4–7, Sun and public hols 4–7 ❚❚ Numerous cafés, bars and restaurants nearby ♿ Few ✋ Inexpensive

GRANADA: MONASTERIO DE LA CARTUJA

The Monasterio de la Cartuja was begun in 1495, but a single patio, planted with orange trees and trim box hedges, is all that survives of the original construction. The current edifice was erected in the 17th century and is flamboyantly baroque, encrusted with lavish ornamentation both inside and out. The art collection is particularly fine, and includes works by Bocanegra, a celebrated Granadino artist of the 17th century, and Juan Sanchez Cotán.

L4 ⊠ Paseo de la Cartuja ☎ 958 16 19 32 ⏰ Apr–end Oct daily 10–1, 4–8; Nov–end Mar daily 10–1, 3–6 ❚❚ None 🚌 8 from city centre ♿ Few ✋ Inexpensive; free on Sun

Soaring interior of Granada's cathedral (left); exterior of the cathedral (below)

The sacristy of the Monasterio de la Cartuja (opposite)

GRANADA: MUSEO ARQUEOLÓGICO Y ETNOLÓGICO DE GRANADA

The Archaeology Museum occupies the handsome Casa de Castril, completed in 1530. Delightfully old-fashioned, it boasts a few curious exhibits, including Roman statues and glassware, and a wonderful Arabic astrolabe (an early navigational device).

✚ L4 ✉ Carrera del Darro 43 ☎ 958 57 54 08 🕐 Tue 2.30–8.30, Wed–Sat 9–8.30, Sun 9–2.30 🍴 None ♿ Few 🖐 Free to Spanish and EU-citizens; otherwise inexpensive

GRANADA: PARQUE DE LAS CIENCIAS

www.parqueciencias.com

This Science Park is on the outskirts of Granada, off the main A338. The park comprises everything from a planetarium and observatory to botanical gardens and a tropical butterfly house. With more than 270 different interactive exhibits, there is plenty to keep the whole family happy.

✚ L4 ✉ Avenida del Mediterráneo s/n ☎ 958 13 19 00 🕐 Tue–Sat 10–7, Sun 10–3

🍴 Snacks 🚌 Local bus connections from the centre of Granada (1, 5 go directly to the Park from the city centre; 4, 10 and 11 head to the nearby Plaza de las Américas) ♿ Good 🖐 Inexpensive; free on Sun

GRANADA: PLAZA BIB-RAMBLA

This is one of the city's prettiest and liveliest squares, dotted with flower stalls and lined with restaurants and bars. It's the perfect spot for some refreshment after a day's sightseeing.

✚ L4 🍴 Cafés, bars and restaurants

LA HERRADURA

www.almunecar.info

This popular family resort occupies a large bay, which arches for two glorious, sandy kilometres between the promontories of Punta de la Mona and Cerro Gordo. It's the perfect destination for fans of all kinds of watersports, with facilities available for everything from scuba-diving to sea-kayaking or windsurfing. For something more sedate, stroll among the yachts of the glossily refurbished Marina del Este.

Scientific facts to absorb at the Parque de las Ciencias

Into the deep—take a scuba-diving lesson at La Herradura

🔲 K6 ✉ Between Almuñécar and Nerja 🍴 Restaurant options are largely limited to beach bars 🚍 Local connections from Nerja and Almuñécar ♿ Few

RINCÓN DE LA VICTORIA
www.rincondelavictoria.es
This modern seaside resort has spruced itself up considerably over the last few years, and now boasts 9km (5.5 miles) of fine, sandy beaches. A wide range of entertainment is available, with facilities for tennis, golf, horse-riding, hot-air ballooning and jeep safaris. According to legend, buried gems still lie hidden in the Cueva del Tesoro (treasure caves).
🔲 J6 🍴 Restaurants 🚍 Regular connections from Málaga ♿ Good ℹ Calle Granada s/n, tel 952 40 77 68

SALOBREÑA
www.ayto-salobrena.org
The old town of Salobreña is perched beautifully on a cliff, with the white-washed villas of the new town spilling down its flanks. The well-kept beaches and stunning clifftop views

remain its biggest draw, but the appealing historic centre shouldn't be missed. Medieval arcades, Mudéjar churches and old-fashioned *tascas* are overlooked by the old Arabic Alcázar (fortress), which offers breath-taking views of the snow-clad peaks of the Sierra Nevada.
🔲 L6 🍴 Restaurants and cafés 🚍 Services from Granada, Almuñécar and Motril ♿ Few ℹ Plaza Goya s/n, tel 958 61 03 14

VÉLEZ MÁLAGA
www.ayto-velezmalaga.es
This thriving market town is presided over by a 13th-century Arabic castle. It's the capital of the Axarquía (▷ 88–89) and known for its abundant fresh produce, sweet Málaga wines and fruity olive oil. These are all available at the weekly market (Thursday). The knotted streets of the old town of Arrabal de San Sebastián are a revelation, redolent of the former Arabic medina.
🔲 J6 🍴 Restaurants and cafés 🚍 Local connections from Torre del Mar and Málaga ♿ Few ℹ Avda Andalucía 52, Torre del Mar, tel 952 54 11 04

Ornate arch at the shrine of the Virgen del Carmen in Rincón de la Victoria

A view from the castle at Salobreña

Tapas Hopping in Granada

This walk introduces you to an endearing custom of Andalucian life, the habit of serving a free *tapa* (snack) with every drink.

DISTANCE: 1.6km (1 mile)   **ALLOW:** 30 minutes plus stops

START

PLAZA DEL CARMEN
L4   4

1 Kick off the night at Puerta del Carmen (No. 1) a new, designer tapas bar with smoky mirrors, wood panels and serious buzz factor. Weave up Calle Mariana Pineda.

2 Stop to take a peek at the Corral del Carbón—the best surviving *caravanserai* (inn) in Spain—before heading northeast along the Calle Reyes Católicos to Plaza Nueva.

3 Plaza Nueva is filled with pavement cafés and leads up onto the Calle Darro to the Cuesta de Chinos, which will get you to the Alhambra (▷ 86–87).

4 For tapas, duck off at the start onto tiny Calle Almiceros where you'll find Bodegas Castañeda (No.1–3). Castañeda is an old favourite, beloved by locals.

END

PLAZA DEL TRIUNFO
L4   C

8 Settle down with some regional wines paired with platters of local cheese and meat. Walk through the gate into the Plaza del Triunfo.

7 This street is known as little Morocco with its kebab shops and *teterías* (tea shops). You then reach the imposing Mudéjar Puerta de Elvira. Just within it you'll find Al Sur de Granada (No. 3), selling exclusively Granada and Alpujarra products.

6 Try toasted almonds and slivers of *jamón Iberico de bellota* washed down with a glass of Fino (a crisp white sherry). When replete turn back on yourself and skirt along Calle Elvira.

5 Hams hang from ancient rafters and the walls are wood panelled.

Shopping

ARTESANÍA ÁRABE CHAMBO

www.artesaniachambo.es
For something really special, consider purchasing something from these craftsmen. For five generations they have been making exquisite marquetry furnishings, using ancient Arabic techniques. Intricate designs are inlaid with mother-of-pearl, polished bone and wood. This authentic workshop can be visited only by appointment.

➕ L4 ✉ Cuesta Chapiz, 70, Granada ☎ 637 40 43 61

BABEL

www.babellibros.com
The largest bookstore in town, with a wide range of titles covering everything from local history to Spanish bestsellers (such as Washington Irving's *Tales of the Alhambra* or Ruiz Zafón's *The Shadow of the Wind*) in translation.

➕ L4 ✉ Calle San Juan de Dios 20, Granada ☎ 958 20 12 98

BOLSOS MONTIEL

All kinds of leather goods are available at this traditional shop, which sells everything from bags and briefcases to wallets, belts and purses. Prices are very reasonable for the quality on offer.

➕ L4 ✉ Calle Principe 3, Granada ☎ 958 26 33 94

LA CARTE DES VINS

www.lacartedesvins.com
This wine shop has a fine selection of the best wines from Spain, France and other countries. They offer a great introduction to wine-tasting course on Thursday evenings (one hour, €10, advance booking essential). There are books, decanters, wine coolers and all kinds of wine-related paraphernalia.

➕ L4 ✉ Calle Navas 29, Granada ☎ 958 22 95 24

CASA PASTELES

www.casapasteles.com
Located on the central Plaza Nueva, this *pastelería* has been going since 1928. You can sit in the café or take away, choosing from a wide selection of local goodies. The cream puffs (*barquillos de crema*) are scrumptious.

➕ L4 ✉ Plaza Larga 1, Granada ☎ 958 27 89 97

SWEET TREATS

There are specialty desserts associated with many of Granada's biggest fiestas: if you are here at Easter, try the *Rosco de San Lázaro*, a circular pastry shell filled with either meringue or cream. Other traditional *Semana Santa* (Holy Week) goodies include *leche frita,* a simple but divine milky treat, as well as *buñuelos*, little puffs filled with cream or chocolate. During Carnival, try *Cuajada de Carnaval*, a yogurt-based pudding that dates back to Arabic times.

CERÁMICA FABRE

Granada's lovely ceramics with their Moorish influences make for wonderful gifts (as well as a salad bowl with a little wow factor). Choose something in the typical blues and greens of the region.

➕ L4 ✉ Plaza Pescadería s/n, Granada ☎ 958 25 81 92

EL CORTE INGLÉS

www.elcorteingles.es
Good all-round department store selling everything from gourmet food stuffs to top-line fashion brands, cosmetics and electronics. Handy when your camera batteries die, you need a new memory card or simply want a bottle of Fino to take home.

➕ L4 ✉ Calle Genil 22, Granada ☎ 958 22 32 40

GONZÁLO REYES MUÑOZ

This is an interesting antique shop, with a wide range of Spanish and Moroccan furniture as well as smaller decorative items. Great for collectors and anyone looking for extra special gifts.

➕ L4 ✉ Calle Mesones (Placeta de Cauchiles 1), Granada ☎ 958 52 32 74

GUITARRERIA GERMÁN PÉREZ BARRANCO

www.guitarreria.com
Beautiful hand-made Spanish guitars and authentic flamenco CDs make this an essential stop for aficionados. Other

flamenco instruments, such as the *cajón*, the box-like drum, are also available. It's not unusual to find virtuoso performers trying out the guitars.
🔸 L4 ✉ Calle Reyes Católicos 47 and Cuesta de Gomerez 10, Granada ☎ 958 22 70 33

LIBRERÍA RECICLAJE
www.reciclajegranada.es
A friendly second-hand bookshop, with an eclectic range of books, CDs, records, DVDs and comics. It's a good place to pick up some holiday reading at a bargain price, or even a dictionary to help out with your Spanish, but you will need to rummage to find the best stuff—perfect for bookshop lovers.
🔸 L4 ✉ San Jerónimo 13, Granada ☎ 958 29 08 70

LOEWE
A branch of the most famous Spanish luxury brand, with a range of designer clothing for men and women, plus plenty of their renowned, beautifully made, leather accessories. There is also a selection of jewellery and fragrances.
🔸 L4 ✉ Calle Angel Ganivet, Granada ☎ 958 22 62 22

MANOS
Small shop selling leather goods and craft-type souvenirs including prints, jewellery and wooden objects.
🔸 K6 ✉ Calle Pintada 9, Nerja ☎ 952 52 11 37

MERCADO MUNICIPAL
Essential for picnic fare as well as gourmet treats such as olive oil, sausages, cheese and wine at local prices.
✉ L4 ✉ Calle San Augustin s/n, Granada ☎ No phone

MIMA
For more than 50 years, Mima has been renowned for its exquisite *mantillas* and shawls, all beautifully hand embroidered. They also sell high-quality fans and *peinetas* (the traditional hair combs) as well as other typical accessories. Check it out for gifts.
🔸 L4 ✉ Calle Reyes Catolicos 18, Granada ☎ 958 22 32 91

TRADITIONAL CRAFTS
Traditional crafts in the Granada region include marquetry, wood carving, ceramics, tapestry-making, embroidered shawls (*mantillas*), leatherwork (including painting on leather), and guitar-making. Many of these arts have their origins in Arabic times, and faithfully follow ancient techniques. There are numerous workshops throughout the city, where you can see artisans at work. Although it is easy to find these crafts in souvenir shops, the tourist office can provide addresses for many of the most celebrated and highly-regarded artisans.

NEPTUNO CENTRE COMERCIAL
For convenient, one-stop shopping, head for this enormous shopping centre. Here, all the famous Spanish brands are gathered under one roof, and there are several cafés, delicatessens for local hams and cheeses, and a supermarket too.
🔸 L4 ✉ Calle Arabial s/n, Granada ☎ 958 52 22 45

NERJA BOOK CENTRE
This huge second-hand bookstore in the centre of town is perfect for picking up some light holiday reading.
🔸 K6 ✉ Calle Granada 30, Nerja ☎ 952 52 09 08

OXIA
Young designer fashion, with labels such as Miss Sixty and Diesel, is the draw at this sleek, minimalist boutique. As well as the best international designers, it also showcases cheaper lines by Spanish designers. Accessories include costume jewellery and shoes.
🔸 L4 ✉ Calle Gracia, Granada ☎ 958 25 84 49

RAIZ
This shop offers a wide selection of handmade, Granadino souvenirs. Everything from ceramics and woodwork, to silver jewellery, glassware and embroidered fabrics.
🔸 L4 ✉ Calle Varela 2, Granada ☎ 958 22 29 29

Entertainment and Activities

ALJIBE SAN MIGUEL (ARAB BATHS)
www.aljibesanmiguel.es
Immerse yourself in the pools at this relaxing, North African-style hammam. Optional treatments include massage and aromatherapy.
➕ L4 ✉ Calle San Miguel Alta 41, Granada ☎ 958 52 28 67 ⏰ Daily 10am–10pm, with sessions every two hours

CINEMA LOS VERGELES
An outdoor cinema (which only operates during the summer months), this is a refreshing way to see the latest releases under the stars. There are four screens and the local tourist information office can tell you what's on. Not all films are screened in V.O. (*versión original*, or undubbed), so check before you go.
➕ L4 ✉ Palencia 22, Granada ☎ 958 81 38 54 ⏰ Check for times

EL COLONO
This popular, 200-hundred-year-old tavern in Nerja is a fun place to have dinner and see lively flamenco performances.
➕ K6 ✉ Calle Granada 6, Nerja ☎ 952 52 18 26 ⏰ Flamenco shows (with set dinner) Wed and Fri; closed Dec to mid-Feb

CUEVA MARIA LA CANASTERA
www.granadainfo.com/canastera/
María Cortés Heredia, a local flamenco legend,

opened this cave in the celebrated *gitano* quarter of Sacromonte over 50 years ago. Now it functions as both museum and live flamenco venue.
➕ L4 ✉ Camino de Sacromonte, 89, Granada ☎ 958 12 11 83 ⏰ Show starts at 10.30pm. Museum 12–2.30, 4.30–7.30

ESHAVIRA
This cavernous bar is a bit difficult to find (down an alley just off Calle Elvira) but worth the trip. This is definitely one for lovers of live jazz and flamenco.
➕ L4 ✉ Calle Postigo de la Cuna 2, Granada ☎ 958 29 08 29 ⏰ Daily 10pm–4am

GRANADA 10
www.granada10.com
This attractive venue occupies a resplendent old theatre, which retains much of its original decoration. In the early

MUSIC AND DANCE FESTIVAL
The Festival Internacional de Música y Danza de Granada (www.granadafestival.org), which takes place in June and July, attracts the city's hottest flamenco stars. Father and daughter act Enrique and Estrella Morente are well worth catching. October sees a clutch of cultural festivals dedicated to everything from world music to theatre. Check with the tourist office for a full programme of events.

evening there are film screenings of cult classics. Later, it is transformed into a nightclub.
➕ L4 ✉ Calle Carcel Baja 10, Granada ☎ 958 22 40 01 ⏰ Cinema screenings 6.30pm (call for details). Club Sun–Thu 12.20am–6am, Fri–Sat 12.30am–7am

EL HUERTO DEL LORO
This curious and original pub occupies a series of interconnected caves, just off the Paseo de los Tristes. In summer, make for the pretty terrace, with its lovely views. DJs play the latest *electronica*.
➕ L4 ✉ Carrera del Darro s/n, Granada ☎ 600 70 00 06 ⏰ Thu–Sat 10pm–4am

MAE WEST
www.grupobribones.com
Mae West is found in the Neptuno shopping centre, the last place you might expect to find the hottest club in town. Expect queues and make sure you're dressed to impress.
➕ L4 ✉ Calle Recogidas (Neptuno Centro Comercial, Granada) ☎ 902 44 24 20 ⏰ Daily midnight–6am

PEATÓN
This tiny, narrow bar is decorated with cult movie posters. It's very popular with locals at weekends and packs out with young Granadinos who enjoy the live indie, pop and rock gigs.
➕ L4 ✉ Calle Sócrates 25, Granada ☎ No phone ⏰ Daily 10pm–3am

PLAZA TUTTI FRUTTI

The haunt of the city's bright young things, this square is filled with numerous bars and clubs. Most have outdoor terraces and the partying goes on until dawn.
🔲 K6 ✉ Plaza Tutti Frutti, Nerja

RINCÓN DE SAN PEDRO

This excellent club, located on the fringes of the Albaicín, offers magical views of the Alhambra. Some of the best local and international DJs play house, electro pop and chill-out music to a mixed gay and straight crowd. Come in the late afternoon for a Moroccan-style mint tea and lounge music. By midnight, the bar is heaving.
🔲 L4 ✉ Carreta del Darro 12, Albaicín, Granada ☎ No phone 🕐 Thu–Sun 4pm–3am

SALA ALBAICÍN

www.flamencoalbayzin.com
One of several traditional flamenco *tablaos* in Granada, this has a wonderful setting next to the Mirador San Cristóbal. This viewpoint, at the top of the Albaicín, offers magnificent views of the Alhambra and the Sierra Nevada. Although geared heavily toward tourists, it attracts top-level performers and is a good option for those being introduced to flamenco. They also

offer a free, 45-minute tour of the Albaicín.
🔲 L4 ✉ Ctra. Murcia s/n, Mirador San Cristóbal, Granada ☎ 958 80 46 46

BUCEO COSTA NERJA

www.nerjadiving.com
This dive centre on Burriana beach offers courses, try-dives and boat trips for certified divers. Visibility can be surprisingly good, and you can admire the varied submarine life along the rocky coast of the Costa Tropical.
🔲 K6 ✉ Playa Burriana, Nerja ☎ 952 25 86 10

SUGAR POP

This is a popular 'after' —the bar that everyone goes to once the clubs

---

ADVENTURE COSTA TROPICAL

Life Adventure (www. lifeadventure.es) is a Nerja-based company offering adventure tourism in the region. Activities include jeep safaris into the Axarquía (▷ 88–89), nature walks and hikes through the *barrancos* (ravines). For horse-riding lessons, beach rides and treks around Salobreña, contact La Herradura Riding Centre (☎ 660 23 13 25; www. herraduraridingcentre.com). The Sierra Nevada has the most southerly ski resort in Europe (www.cetursa.es),with 60km (40 miles) of pistes offering views of the Mediterranean.

---

have closed in order to continue the party. Retro-cool décor and DJs playing pop, electro and indie-pop have made it a favourite with hip young Granadinos.
🔲 L4 ✉ Calle Gran Capitan 25, Granada ☎ No phone 🕐 Wed–Sat 1am–6am

TABERNA FLAMENCA RICARDO DE LA JUANA, ALMUÑÉCAR

The only properly authentic flamenco folk club or *peña* on the Costa Tropical (or the Costa del Sol for that matter), this place oozes atmosphere from its rustic, wood beamed ceilings right down to its colourful tiled walls.
🔲 L6 ✉ Calle Manila 4, Almuñécar ☎ 958 63 51 98 🕐 Check for times of shows

TEATRO ALHAMBRA

Plays here are mainly in Spanish, but the language barrier doesn't matter for dance. It's a reliable venue for top quality flamenco, ballet and classical and jazz concerts.
🔲 L4 ✉ Calle Molinos 56, Granada ☎ 958 02 80 00 🕐 Check for times and programme of concerts

WINDSURF LA HERRADURA

www.windsurflaherradura.com
Windsurfing, surfboard and kayak hire and lessons on the beach.
🔲 K6 ✉ Paseo Maritimo 34, La Herradura ☎ 958 64 01 43

Restaurants

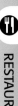
PRICES

Prices are approximate, based on a 3-course meal for one person.

€€€ over €45
€€   €25–€45
€   under €25

BAR RESTAURANTE PESETAS (€)

Classical Spanish tapas with bucket loads of fresh fish and seafood on a roof-top terrace in the old town.
🔼 L6 ✉ Calle Bóveda 11, Salobreña ☎ 958 61 01 82 🕐 Daily lunch and dinner

LOS BARRILES (€)

The charming old-school tapas bar is a great place to start the night. Try sherry straight from the barrel and flaming chori-zos (*chorizo al infierno*).
🔼 K6 ✉ Calle Carabeo 5, Nerja ☎ No phone 🕐 Daily dinner

BODEGA FRANCISCO (€)

Great little tapas bar in the old town serving all the classics: thin slivers of *jamón* (ham); croquettes and little fried fish. All washed down with clean, crisp *copas* of *fino* (dry sherry from Jerez).
🔼 L6 ✉ Calle Real 14, Almuñécar ☎ 958 63 01 68 🕐 Daily lunch and dinner; closed Jan–end Feb

BODEGA SAINT GERMAIN (€€)

This bustling wine bar is reminiscent of a Parisian brasserie, with its battered furnishings and huge wine-coolers. The superb wine list features lots of small boutique wineries. They are perfectly accom-panied by inventive tapas: try the ostrich with onion confit or the quail and *foie milhoja*.
🔼 L4 ✉ Calle Postigo Velutti 4, Granada ☎ No phone 🕐 Daily lunch and dinner

LA BODEGUILLA (€)

www.labodeguillafrigiliana.com A village classic, this little townhouse with its terrace covered in giant rubber trees is run by Rosario and her four daughters. The food is simple and typical of the region: try pork chops served with *papas a lo pobre* (pota-toes with onions and peppers) and fried eggs.

HISTORY OF TAPAS

The word *tapa* literally means 'lid', and recalls the old custom of covering drinks with a piece of bread to keep the flies off. According to legend, the first elaborate tapas began when the king of Spain demanded a cup of wine in a tavern near Cádiz. When the usual slice of stale bread appeared, a courtier roared 'Can't you do some-thing better than that for the king of Spain?' A slice of ham and cheese was duly placed on top, marking the start of a most convivial and popular tradition.

🔼 K6 ✉ Calle Chorruelo 7, Frigiliana ☎ 952 53 41 16 🕐 Daily lunch and dinner

CASA JULIO (€)

Delightfully battered and old-fashioned, Casa Julio prepares some of the best *fritura de pescado* (small, deep-fried fish) in the city. Eat at the crowded bar, or try and grab one of the few pavement tables.
🔼 L4 ✉ Calle Hermosa 5, Granada ☎ No phone 🕐 Daily lunch and dinner

CASA LUQUE (€€€)

www.casaluque.com With a spectacular location on the Balcón de Europa, and a breezy terrace overlooking the sea, this family-run restaurant is a local classic. Try Andalucian classics prepared with an original touch.
🔼 K6 ✉ Plaza de Cavana 2, Nerja ☎ 952 52 10 04 🕐 Lunch and dinner; closed Sun lunch, Wed and Jan

LA CEPA (€€–€€€)

This upmarket tapas bar and restaurant offers a wide range of wines from all over Spain to accompany the sophisticated food. Don't miss the aubergine stuffed ravioli and kobe beef steaks with tasty *Bierzo pimientos* (sweet peppers) and figs.
🔼 L4 ✉ Calle San Matías 4, Granada ☎ 958 22 33 06 🕐 Daily lunch and dinner

CHIKITO (€)

www.restaurantechikito.com
Chikito is a large, friendly tavern, with a down-to-earth bar for tapas, and a separate rustically decorated dining area for more substantial fare. House specialties include *rabo de toro* (ox tail), and traditional desserts.

➕ L4 ✉ Plaza del Campillo 9, Granada ☎ 958 22 33 64 ⏰ Lunch and dinner; closed Wed

CUNINI (€–€€€)

This celebrated restaurant has a wonderful terrace out on the square, but locals prefer to crowd around the bar and tuck into the tapas. Cunini is especially good for fabulously fresh shellfish and classic Mediterranean fish dishes. Charming décor.

➕ L4 ✉ Plaza de la Pescadería 1, Granada ☎ 958 25 07 77 ⏰ Lunch and dinner; closed Sun dinner

DE COSTA A COSTA (€–€€)

An attractive, modern restaurant with nautically themed décor, this specializes in refined seafood tapas and *raciones* (large tapas portions).

➕ L4 ✉ Calle Ancha de Gracia 3, Lojo, Granada ☎ 958 52 31 37 ⏰ Lunch and dinner; closed Mon

GARDEN RESTAURANT (€€)

This deeply romantic outdoor restaurant spills over terraces, offering spellbinding views over the mountains and down to the sea. The tapas menu is imaginative, with lots of Moorish influenced dishes, fresh salads and a particularly good wine list.

➕ K6 ✉ Frigiliana, (well-signposted from the village, but no car access) ☎ 952 53 31 85 ⏰ Lunch and dinner; closed Tue

HELADERÍA TIGGIANI (€)

Open since 1961 this ice cream shop is a cut above average serving inventive cones such as chocolate with chilli and passion fruit with avocado.

➕ L4 ✉ Plaza Bib-Rambla 11, Granada ☎ 958 25 28 11 ⏰ Open all day

HOTEL LA TARTANA (€€–€€€)

www.hotellatartana.com
La Tartana has beautiful

A TASTE OF AFRICA

In and around Granada the influence of the Moors can be tasted in a myriad of ways—and not just in the kebab houses, cake shops and *teterías* that have sprung up. Arabic influenced dishes such as fried aubergines drizzled with honey, *migas* (fried breadcrumbs used much like couscous), the prevalence of cumin, coriander and saffron, and spiced-sugar cakes like *roscos* and nougat, all form part of the culinary culture of the region.

---

mature gardens for sipping a pre-dinner aperitif, and the excellent menu offers modern American and Pan-Asian cuisine served with a touch of panache.

➕ K6 ✉ A7-E15 exit 14, Urbanización San Nicolás, La Herradura ☎ 958 64 05 35 ⏰ Mon–Sat dinner

EL HUERTO DE JUAN RANAS (€€€)

www.restaurantejuanranas.com
One of the smartest of the Carmen restaurants (Carmens are the traditional Albaicín villas), this boasts spectacular views of the Alhambra and the Sierra Nevada.

➕ L4 ✉ Calle Atarazana 8, Granada ☎ 958 28 69 25 ⏰ Terrace Tue–Sun 11am–midnight (dining room from 8pm)

LANSANG (€€)

This sleek restaurant is one of the best places in Spain for authentic Thai and Laotian food. Most products are sourced locally, and key ingredients like lemon grass are grown specially.

➕ K6 ✉ Calle Málaga 12, Nerja ☎ 952 52 80 53 ⏰ Tue–Sat lunch and dinner, Sun dinner; closed Sun lunch and Mon

MESÓN LOS PALANCOS (€€)

Just below the castle with lovely views from the terrace, this friendly restaurant serves hearty fare such as Iberian pork

steaks, rabbit stew and roast goat. A photo of footballing legend David Beckham, who has eaten here, adorns the wall.
➕ J3 ✉ Plaza de la Paz s/n, Zuheros ☎ 957 69 45 38 ⏱ Daily lunch and dinner

MESÓN RIOFRÍO (€€)

A comfortable country inn housed in a handsome *cortijo*, with rustic decoration and a fine selection of local specialties. You shouldn't miss the local cheeses, perfect with a glass of Andalucian wine.
➕ J4 ✉ Plaza de San Isidro s/n, Loja ☎ 958 32 13 61 ⏱ Daily lunch and dinner

MIRADOR DE CERRO GORDO (€€€)

www.miradorcerrogordo.com
Worth a visit for the views alone, this restaurant perches on the cliffs above the beaches of the Costa Tropical. The food is creative Mediterranean with Asian accents. A series of terraces under the stars add a magical touch.
➕ K6 ✉ Ctra. Vieja de Málaga, Nerja ☎ 958 34 90 99 ⏱ Jun–end Sep daily from 11am for light meals, plus a-la-carte dinner; Oct–mid Dec and Mar–end May Tue–Sat from 11am for light meals, plus a-la-carte dinner, Sun lunch; closed mid-Dec–end Feb (phone ahead early/late season to check open)

MUSEO DEL VINO (€)

Possibly one of the smallest museums in the world, this will take you about 5 minutes to get around,

but considerably longer to sip the local wines and nibble tapas. Don't miss a glass of the sweet Jarel (a famous local moscatel).
➕ K6 ✉ Avenida Constitución 6, Cómpeta ☎ 952 55 33 14 ⏱ Opening times vary, call for details

EL PEÑON (€€)

www.elpenon.es
One of the most famous restaurants in the region, this has a fabulous location on the rocks. Beautifully fresh fish and seafood, and stunning views make it well worth a detour.
➕ L6 ✉ Playa del Peñón, Paseo Marítimo, Salobreña ☎ 958 61 05 38 ⏱ Daily lunch and dinner; closed Sep–Jun

SCARLETTA'S (€€–€€€)

The town's trendiest restaurant, this attracts a hip, young crowd. Come for cocktails on the roof terrace, groovy tunes and top-notch fusion cuisine.

COLD SOUP

The classic, chilled Andalucian soup is gazpacho, a wonderfully refreshing concoction made with tomatoes, pepper, cucumbers and garlic. In Córdoba, they prepare *salmorejo*, which also has a tomato base but is thickened with breadcrumbs and topped with chopped boiled egg and ham. You could also try *ajo blanco*, a delicate soup flavoured with almonds and garlic.

➕ K6 ✉ Calle Cristo 38, Nerja ☎ 952 52 00 11 ⏱ Daily lunch and dinner

SEVILLA (€€€)

This long-established local restaurant has a magnificent summer terrace right in front of the cathedral. The interior is elegant and the menu features refined regional cuisine.
➕ L4 ✉ Calle Oficios 12, Granada ☎ 958 22 12 23 ⏱ Lunch and dinner; closed Sun dinner, Mon lunch (Jul–Aug Sun and Mon)

EL TRAGALUZ (€€€)

Arguably Granada's best restaurant, El Tragaluz offers a very interesting menu that fuses East and West culinary traditions. The tagine is highly recommended. It's popular with local artists and writers, and the ambience is relaxed and intimate.
➕ L4 ✉ Calle Nevot 26, Granada ☎ 958 22 29 24 ⏱ Tue–Sat lunch and dinner, Sun lunch

VENTA DE ALFARNATE (€€€)

www.ventadealfarnate.es
This rustic old coaching inn is a real delight. The warren of rooms with wood beams and open hearths has barely changed in centuries. The menu is timeless, with local fare like rabbit casserole with fennel and wild boar stew.
➕ L4 ✉ Antique Carretera de Málaga-Granada km 513, Axarquía ☎ 952 75 93 88 ⏱ Tue–Sun 10–6

The Costa del Sol offers a wide range of
accommodation, from plush resorts with
every imaginable facility to charming rural
hotels. Some of Spain's finest *paradors*
(the state-run hotels, often in historic
buildings) can also be found.

Where to Stay

Introduction

Whether you want a five-star spa resort on the beach, or a simple mountain inn, the Costa del Sol has it all. Book early for the high season (mid–July to end–August), as prices can double. During the rest of the year, particularly in the winter, there are some extraordinary bargains to be had.

Types of Accommodation

Spanish hotels are classified, regularly inspected and awarded 1 to 5 stars (*estrellas*). These stars refer to facilities and don't take into account charm or service. *Hostales* are often hard to distinguish from small hotels and can be better value for money. They are graded from 1 to 3 stars: a 3-star *hostal* is generally on a par with a 2-star hotel. *Pensiones* are family-run establishments with simple rooms that may or may not have private bathrooms. There are numerous self-catering options available on the Costa del Sol. You can find a comprehensive directory of all types of accommodation on the following official tourism websites: www.andalucia.org and www.visitacostadelsol.com.

Rural Tourism

Rural tourism has taken off in recent years, and numerous accommodation options can be found in the hinterland. Holidays on working farms are becoming increasingly common, and Andalucía has a fine selection of historic *haciendas* (grand country hrtouses) and *cortijos* (farms)—there are listings at www.andalucia.org. For charming self-catering cottages, try Rustic Blue (www.rusticblue.com) or Top Rural (www.toprural.com).

BEST *PARADORS* ON THE COSTA DEL SOL

Many of these state-run hotels are located in magnificent historic buildings, see www.parador.es. Book well in advance for the Granada and the modern Ronda *parador*, which overlooks the famous Puente Nuevo. Other beautiful *paradors* can be found in Arcos de la Frontera and Carmona. The modern Nerja *parador* has a spectacular clifftop location, as does Málaga's Parador de Gibralfaro.

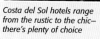

Costa del Sol hotels range from the rustic to the chic—there's plenty of choice

Budget Hotels

PRICES

Expect to pay up to €100 per night for a double room in a budget hotel.

LA BOTICA

www.laboticadevejer.com
Stylish, simple and intimate, this occupies an old pharmacy tucked away in Véjer's enchanting old quarter. Beaches are a short drive away.
⊞ C8 ⊠ Calle Canalejas 13, Véjer de la Frontera ☎ 956 45 02 25

CASA CONDE DE PINOFIEL

www.hotelpinofiel.com
An 18th-century baroque palace, offering classically decorated rooms overlooking a central patio in the heart of the town.
⊞ H5 ⊠ La Tercia 10, Antequera ☎ 952 84 24 64

CASA DE FEDERICO

www.casadefederico.com
A delightful little inn, with stylish rooms decorated with local artwork. Balconies offer views of the whitewashed rooftops of the Alabaicín.
⊞ L4 ⊠ Calle Horno Marina 13, Granada ☎ 958 20 85 34

ENFRENTE ARTE

www.enfrentearte.com
Quirky decoration, a relaxed ambience and rambling tropical gardens make this a genuine charmer. Wonderful views over the Sierra.
⊞ F6 ⊠ Calle Real 40, Ronda ☎ 952 87 90 88

LA ESTRELLA DE TARIFA

www.laestrelladetarifa.com
In the heart of the old quarter, this appealing little guesthouse has a handful of simple rooms with Moroccan-style décor.
⊞ D9 ⊠ San Rosendo 4, Tarifa ☎ 956 68 19 85 (mobile 670 73 97 23)

LA FRUCTUOSA

www.lafructuosa.com
This lovely rural hotel has five spacious, light-filled rooms offering beautiful views of the Sierra de Ronda and down to the coast, and two cottages for rent. There's a good restaurant with good views over to Africa and Gibraltar.
⊞ E7 ⊠ Calle Convento 67, Gaucín ☎ 952 15 10 72

ROOM-MATE HOTELS

Room-Mate Hotels offer contemporary style on a budget. It's a medium-sized chain, with hotels in several Spanish and international cities. Their hotels are all friendly, fabulously decorated and well-equipped with modern amenities such as WiFi. Breakfast is always included (unlike most Spanish hotels), and prices are very modest. On the Costa del Sol, you'll find two Room-Mate hotels in Málaga (Lola and Laurios), and three in Granada (Migueletes, Leo, Shalma). More information at www.room-matehotels.es.

HOTEL LA TARTANA

www.hotellatartana.com
This beautifully restored mansion set in mature gardens oozes charm and tranquility. There are eight rooms, all classically decorated, and set around a typical Andalucian central patio complete with fountain. The restaurant (▷ 105) is outstanding.
⊞ K6 ⊠ Urbanización San Nicolás, La Herradura ☎ 958 64 05 35

HOTEL PALACIO BLANCO

www.palacioblanco.com
A very chic, boutique hotel in La Axarquía, (▷ 88–89) located in a historic *palacete* that offers four-star amenities, stylish rooms and a small pool for an incredibly modest price.
⊞ J6 ⊠ Calle Félix Lomas, 4, Velez-Malaga ☎ 952 54 91 74

HOTEL ZUHAYRA

www.zercahoteles.com
This classic, Spanish country hotel is located in a pretty village. There's a very decent restaurant.
⊞ J3 ⊠ Calle Mirador 10, Zuheros ☎ 957 69 46 93

POSADA MORISCA

www.laposadamorisca.com
These little white cottages on the mountainside have been converted into a beautiful rural retreat. Elegant, individually decorated rooms, a swimming pool and sublime views.
⊞ K6 ⊠ Calle Loma de la Cruz s/n, Frigiliana ☎ 952 53 41 51

Mid-Range Hotels

PRICES

Expect to pay between €100–€200 per night for a double room in a mid-range hotel.

ALBERO LODGE
www.alberolodge.com
A perfect, beachside retreat, this traditional, beautiful villa has just 5 individually decorated rooms overlooking a pool and lush gardens.
➕ F7 ✉ Urbanización Finca La Cancelada Támesis 16, Estepona ☎ 952 88 07 00

ALCAZÁR DE LA REINA
www.alcazar-reina.es
In Carmona's enchanting old quarter, this handsome hotel in an 18th-century mansion has a small garden, a good restaurant, an outdoor pool, and a pleasant plant-filled patio.
➕ D3 ✉ Calle Hermana Concepción Orellana 2, Carmona ☎ 954 19 62 00

AMANHAVIS
www.amanhavis.com
There's a North African feel in this romantic, traditionally tiled hotel-restaurant, in the mountain village of Benahavis. It's close to Marbella and Puerto Banús but feels a world away.
➕ F7 ✉ Calle Pilar 3, Benahavis ☎ 952 85 60 26

THE BEACH HOUSE
www.beachhouse.nu
A gorgeous, whitewashed villa right on the seafront, with sleek, minimalist interior design. There's an outdoor pool, with a terrace for alfresco breakfasts and cocktails in the evening.
➕ H7 ✉ Urbanización El Chaparral, N-340 km 203, Mijas Costa ☎ 952 49 45 40

CARMEN DE COBERTIZO
www.carmendelcobertizo.es
One of the most romantic hotels in the whole region, this occupies a magnificent 16th-century Carmen in the Albaicín. A central patio is overlooked by an original wooden gallery, and there's a tiny, luxuriant garden with a plunge pool. The Alhambra Suite offers breathtaking views of the palace.
➕ L4 ✉ Calle Cobertizo de Santa Inés 6, Granada ☎ 958 22 76 52

CASA CINCO
www.hotelcasacinco.com
Each of the five rooms

COUNTRY HOTELS

Andalucía has some extraordinary little country hotels, which ooze charm and tranquillity. Many of them can be found on the Internet: there is an excellent selection at Inns of Spain (www.innsofspain.com) and through Rusticae (www.rusticae.es). You could also try www.toprural.com, which lists rural hotels and inns, as well as self-catering accommodation.

at this ultra-stylish little inn is dedicated to one of the five senses, all sleekly decorated with a fashionable mixture of antique and contemporary furnishings. Thoughtful extras include bathroom goodies from Pascal Morabito.
➕ C8 ✉ Calle Sancho IV el Bravo 6, Véjer de la Frontera ☎ 956 45 50 29

CASA DE CARMONA
www.casadecarmona.com
A 16th-century palace, beautifully furnished by its aristocratic owner with antiques, this also boasts a pool and a luxuriant, Arabic-style garden. The restaurant, in the former stables, is perfect for a romantic dinner.
➕ D3 ✉ Plazuela Lasso 1, Carmona ☎ 954 19 10 00

CHANCILLERÍA
www.hotelchancilleria.com
This elegant new boutique hotel makes use of the latest eco-friendly technology, and most of the hotel is wheelchair accessible. Located in the heart of Jerez's gipsy quarter, the elegant rooms are decorated with modern monochromatic prints. There's a fine restaurant and very attentive service.
➕ C6 ✉ Calle Chancillería 21, Jerez de La Frontera ☎ 956 30 10 38

HACIENDA LA HERRIZA
www.laherriza.com
A series of ochre-painted

villas in the hills beyond Gaucín, this luxurious complex offers a choice of self-catering cottages or suites, all spacious and exquisitely decorated. There's a restaurant, and numerous activities can be arranged if you like, from horse-riding to fishing.

➕ E7 ✉ Crta. Gaucín–El Colmenar km 6, Gaucín ☎ 951 06 82 00

HOTEL AMADEUS

www.hotelamadeussevilla.com
Book early for a room at this budget favourite, which occupies a beautifully tiled, traditional Andalucian townhouse in the old centre.

➕ C3 ✉ Calle Farnesio 6, Sevilla ☎ 954 50 14 43

HOTEL LOS CARACOLES

www.hotelloscaracoles.com
This attractive and original hotel is set in a series of snail-shaped bungalows (*caracoles* means snails) set in rolling hills. Prices plummet in the low season.

➕ K6 ✉ Ctra Frigiliana-Torrox km 4.5, Frigiliana ☎ 952 03 06 80

HOTEL MOLINA LARIO

www.hotelmolinalario.com
On one of the best shopping streets in the heart of Málaga, this hotel offers contemporary rooms and excellent service.

➕ c1 ✉ Calle Molina Lario 20–222, Málaga ☎ 952 06 20 02

HOTEL SAN GABRIEL

www.hotelsangabriel.com
A handsome 18th-century mansion in Ronda's old quarter, the San Gabriel is a welcoming hotel with classically decorated rooms, a library crammed with books on the historic city, and a pretty plant-filled patio.

➕ F6 ✉ Calle Marqués de Moctezuma 19, Ronda ☎ 952 19 03 92

HURRICANE HOTEL

www.hotelhurricane.com
A relaxed fashionable retreat overlooking Tarifa's famous golden beaches, the Hurricane is a whitewashed, Moroccan-style villa set in lush tropical gardens, with a gym, two pools and a sauna.

CAVE ROOMS

For a truly different holiday, consider renting one of the caves in Sacromonte, the lofty gipsy quarter of Granada. These caves have been inhabited for centuries, but some have been refurbished to offer an alternative to traditional accommodation. Apartments Sacromonte (www.granadainfo.com/sacro) and Cuevas de Abanico (www.el-abanico.com) offer a range of cave dwellings, some with private terraces or gardens. The caves maintain a constant cool temperature throughout the year—a bonus in the searing heat of summer.

➕ D9 ✉ Ctra. Nac. 340 km 78, Tarifa ☎ 956 68 49 19

MOLINO DEL ARCO

www.hotelmolinodelarco.com
Serenity reigns at this exquisitely converted mill, in the hills 8km (5 miles) from the middle of Ronda. Cool pastel shades dominate the lovely interior, and the terraces offer incomparable views of the olive groves.

➕ F6 ✉ Partido de los Frontones s/n, 29400 Ronda, Málaga ☎ 952 11 40 17

MOLINO DE SANTILLÁN

www.molinodesantillan.es
A family-run hotel in the hills above Málaga, this charmingly converted former mill is the perfect rural retreat. There's a swimming pool, but all kinds of activities can also be arranged, including golf, mountain-biking, horse-riding and hiking.

➕ J6 ✉ Carretera de Macharaviaya km 3, Rincón de la Victoria ☎ 952 40 09 49 🕒 Closed 15 Nov–15 Feb

LA VILLA MARBELLA

www.lavillamarbella.com
There are just four chic suites at this delightful, ivy-clad inn in Marbella's old quarter. The décor takes its inspiration from Asia, with richly coloured silk cushions and rattan furnishings.

➕ G7 ✉ Calle Príncipe 10, Marbella ☎ 952 76 62 20

Luxury Hotels

BARCELÓ LA BOBADILLA

www.la-bobadilla.com
Hidden away in the mountains halfway between Málaga and Granada, this enormous *finca* is set in extensive gardens. The superb facilities include two fine restaurants, a brand new spa and a gigantic outdoor pool. It is an excellent choice for families.
➕ J4 ✉ Carretera Salinas-Villanueva de Tapia (A-333), km 65.5, Loja ☎ 958 32 18 61

CASA NO.7

www.casanumero7.com
An exclusive hotel with just a handful of rooms, this exquisite retreat has all the intimacy of a private home. Antiques and objets d'art from the aristocratic owner decorate the rooms. A gem.
➕ C3 ✉ Calle Vírgenes 7, Sevilla ☎ 954 22 15 81

LAS DUNAS BEACH HOTEL & SPA

www.las-dunas.com
Overlooking the beach, this ultra-luxurious, modern resort offers all-suite accommodation. There are several restaurants, every imaginable sports facility, a fabulous spa and a kids' club.
➕ F7 ✉ Carretera N-340 Cádiz-Málaga km 163.5, Estepona ☎ 952 80 94 00

DUQUES DE MEDINACELI

www.prestigehw.com
A magnificent 18th-century mansion in the heart of El Puerto de Santa María has become an outstanding luxury hotel. It's surrounded by magnificent tropical gardens and is filled with antiques and archaeological finds.
➕ B6 ✉ Plaza de los Jazmines 2, El Puerto de Santa María ☎ 956 86 07 77

HACIENDA BENAZUZA

www.elbullihotel.com
Ferran Adriá of the world's most famous restaurant, El Bullí, is behind this magnificent country hotel. The historic *hacienda* dates back to Arabic times, and is surrounded by

gardens and terraces. The restaurants are outstanding.
➕ C3 ✉ Sanlúcar La Mayor, Sevilla ☎ 955 73 33 44

HOTEL PUENTE ROMANO

www.puenteromano.com
Set around the genuine 1st century Roman bridge that gives the hotel its name, the Puente Romano sits in lush gardens. It's an integral part of the local social scene with an excellent tennis club and summer concerts.
➕ G7 ✉ Bulevar Principe Alfonso von Hohenloche, Marbella ☎ 952 82 09 00

KEMPINSKI

www.kempinski-estepona.com
Part of the German chain, this spectacular hotel is arranged over terraces on the beachfront, surrounded by tropical gardens with cascades and palm trees. There's a wide choice of restaurants and sports' facilities.
➕ F7 ✉ Carretera N-340 Cádiz-Málaga km 159, Estepona ☎ 952 80 95 00

MARBELLA CLUB HOTEL, GOLF CLUB AND SPA

www.marbellaclub.com
The Marbella Club is one of the most prestigious hotels on the Costa del Sol. Join the rich and famous at the Beach Club, on the greens at the private golf course, or be pampered at the spa.
➕ G7 ✉ Bulevar Principe Alfonso von Hohenlohe, Marbella ☎ 952 82 22 11

The gateway to the Costa del Sol, Málaga's airport is one of the busiest in Spain, with flights from across the globe. Public transport is patchy—excellent in some regions, but slow or non-existent in certain inland regions. A car is useful for exploring.

Planning Ahead

When to Go

Spain is blessed with the highest number of sunlight hours in Europe. Tourist crowds tend to decrease in winter, and swell in summer, when the heat can be intense and the beaches over-crowded. Many restaurants and resorts close up and rest before and after the high season.

TIME
Ⓛ Spain is six hours ahead of New York, nine hours ahead of Los Angeles and one hour ahead of the UK.

AVERAGE DAILY MAXIMUM TEMPERATURES

JAN	FEB	MAR	APR	MAY	JUN	JUL	AUG	SEP	OCT	NOV	DEC
16°F	17°F	19°F	21°F	24°F	28°F	30°F	30°F	28°F	24°F	20°F	17°F
8°C	9°C	10°C	11°C	13°C	19°C	20°C	20°C	19°C	13°C	12°C	9°C

Spring (mid-March to mid-June) is on par with autumn as the most pleasant time to visit, though rain can often be expected in April.

Summer (mid-June to mid-September) can get uncomfortably hot in the interior, especially in and around Córdoba and Sevilla.

Autumn (mid-September to mid-December) temperatures are warm to moderate, and many still bathe in the sea right up until early December.

Winter (mid-December to mid-March) can be a good time to visit if your focus is more cultural, though it can get very cold in the mountainous areas around Granada.

WHAT'S ON

The Andalucian tourist office publishes an excellent free guide, *52 and a half weeks*, available in several languages. Pick it up from any tourist office. It lists all the festivals in the region, from tiny rural fairs to big events.

December/January *Navidad* (Christmas): Celebrations start early December and end on 5 January with the *Cabalgata de Reyes*, or Procession of the Three Kings. Most towns and villages set up a special Christmas market.

February *Carnaval*: Held all over the region, with the biggest celebration in Cádiz.

April *Semana Santa* (Holy Week): The archetypal image of the hooded, cross-dragging penitent is common all along the Costa del Sol during Easter week–the largest in Granada and Sevilla.

Feria de Abril (11 days mid-April): The region's most famous fiesta is celebrated in Sevilla, with all night *sevillana* dancing and displays of the famous Andalucian horses.

June *San Barnabe* (a week long festival from 11 July): Marbella celebrates its patron saint. On the night of San Juan (24 June) people head to the Costa's beaches, and celebrate the summer solstice with fireworks and partying.

July On 16 July the entire coast around Málaga honours Carmen, the patron saint of fisherman, with colourful maritime festivities.

August The biggest of the region's numerous summer fiestas is in Málaga, with concerts on the beach and huge fairy-lit fairground attractions on the city's outskirts (from 19 August).

September *Biennale de Flamenco*: Every second year Málaga is wrapped in *duende*.

November *All Saint's Day* (1 November): The Spanish honour the dead and relatives clean and pretty up the graves of their ancestors with floral offerings.

Costa del Sol Online

www.visitcostadelsol.com
Málaga region's official tourism website, with loads of destination information and monthly cultural calendars. In English, German, French and Japanese.

www.granadatur.com
Granada's official tourism site with lots of maps and leaflets to download and plenty of information on the Alhambra, the city's most famous site.

www.andalucia.com
Accommodation, weather, festivals, gastronomy and sports information. Also has a blog where you can post questions to other users before you arrive. In English.

www.absolutemagazine.com
The on-line version of the luxury lifestyle magazine *Absolute Marbella* has a good selection of articles aimed at the Costa's rich and famous, plus some good information on hot local hotels, restaurants and shopping.

www.surinenglish.com
The on-line, English language version of *Diario Sur*, Málaga's top selling newspaper, with local news, community events, what's on and a classified section.

www.flamenco-world.com
Everything you always wanted to know about flamenco but were afraid to ask, with festival and concert programmes, interviews, reviews and a helpful guide to the history and various elements of the *cante jondo*. In English.

www.portaltaurino.com
Exhaustive website on the art of bullfighting, with calendar of *corridas*, profiles of bullfighters and breeders, history, culture, interviews and even a gossip page. Some articles in English.

GOOD TRAVEL SITES

www.renfe.es/ingles
The official site of the Spanish National Railways, with an English-speaking option.

www.wunderground.com
Accurate weather forecasting.

www.quierohotel.com
A Spain-based hotel booking site, with hotels all over the country and sections by theme, such as golf, beach and rural hotels. In English.

www.parador.es
The official site of the state-run *parador* network: luxury hotels located in historic buildings. Special web-only offers available.

www.iberia.es
Spain's national airline. On-line booking available with special offers.

www.vueling.com
This Spanish low-cost carrier flies to many destinations in the Costa del Sol, including Sevilla, Málaga and Granada.

WIRELESS MÁLAGA

Málaga, the capital of the Costa del Sol, is the first Spanish city to offer free wireless internet connection, which is available in 80 per cent of the metropolitan district. So, don't forget your laptop.

Getting There

ENTRY REQUIREMENTS

● Anyone entering Spain must have a valid passport (or official identity card for EU nationals). Visa requirements are subject to change, so check before making your reservations.

● Passengers on all flights to and from Spain are required to supply advance passenger information (API) to the Spanish authorities—full names, nationality, date of birth and travel document details, namely a passport number. This information is compulsory. Travel agents can collect this information at the time of booking, or it can be given to staff at check-in desks. Online, give the information at the time of booking.

CUSTOMS

● The limits for non-EU visitors are 200 cigarettes or 50 cigars, or 250g of tobacco; 1 litre of spirits (over 22 per cent) or 2 litres of fortified wine, 2 litres of still wine; 50ml of perfume. Travellers under 18 are not entitled to the tobacco and alcohol allowances.

● The guidelines for EU residents (for personal use) are 800 cigarettes, 200 cigars, 1kg of tobacco; 10 litres of spirits (over 22 per cent), 20 litres of aperitifs, 90 litres of wine, of which 60 can be sparkling wine, 110 litres of beer.

AIRPORTS

Most flights from the UK arrive in Málaga. Flights from other Spanish cities and some European destinations (including the UK) also arrive at Sevilla, Granada and Jerez de la Frontera airports. For general information, including flight arrivals and departures ☎ 902 40 47 04; www.aena.es.

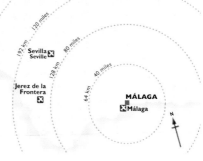

BY AIR

Málaga Airport (www.malaga-airport-guide.com) is located 8km (5 miles) west of the city and next to the A7 autopista, the main highway that connects Costa del Sol destinations to the east and west. Taxis are available outside terminals 1 (arrivals) and 2 (departures) and should cost between €15 and €20 to Málaga city. Number L-19 buses leave every half hour (7am to midnight) from outside terminal 2 to Málaga, finishing at the Paseo del Parque, the city's central hub (see www.emtmalaga.es). Daily buses also connect the airport with Marbella (see www.ctsa-portillo.com). Airport expansion currently underway will include rail services from the airport to various coastal towns. Sevilla's airport is serviced by a half-hourly bus service (6.15am–11pm) to the city centre, or a taxi should cost about €20 for the 10km (6-mile) trip. From Jerez de la Frontera airport, a taxi will cost €15 for the 5km (3-mile) trip to the city and in Granada the bus service ties in with flight arrivals (see www.autocaresjosegonzalez.com); a taxi will cost about €25 for the 16km (10-mile) journey—check the meter is on.

BY BUS

All major destinations in the region are serviced by daily buses from Barcelona, Madrid and Valencia. Málaga's bus station (☎ 952 35 00 61) is located in the Paseo de los Tilos, 15 minutes walk from the city centre.

BY CAR

Drivers access the Costa del Sol region via the Spanish system of toll motorways (*autopistas*) and/or highways (*autovías*). The 540km (335-mile) journey from Madrid to Málaga is done on the modern AP4 motorway. From Barcelona, the 1,000km (620-mile) journey follows the eastern coast of Spain on the AP7, passing through Valencia and Alicante and is more comfortably taken over two days. (With an abundance of hotels and located at the halfway mark, Benidorm makes a good place to spend the night.) From Málaga, the AP7 continues both east and westwards along the coast, connecting popular destinations such as Marbella, Torremolinos and Nerja. Drivers heading to smaller villages along the coast can also use the prettier, yet slower, Autovía del Mediterraneo as far west as Cádiz.

BY TRAIN

Trains to the smaller towns and villages of the Costa del Sol are limited but Renfe, Spain's national train service, has services to the region's major cities from the north. The high-speed AVE train zips to Sevilla and Málaga from Madrid in a couple of hours. Other destinations, such as Jerez de la Frontera, Málaga and Granada, are serviced by slower, more picturesque services from Madrid, Valencia and Barcelona. Special train 'hotels', such as Elipsos Trenhotels (www.elipsos.com), offer sleeping cabins—a stylish way to travel; Talgos high speed trains are usually used for day journeys; and Avant trains connect Málaga, Sevilla and Córdoba. For information or to book online see www.renfe.es (☎ 902 24 02 02 from inside Spain or ☎ 902 24 34 02 from elsewhere).

SENSIBLE PRECAUTIONS

● Never leave luggage and other valuables on the seats of cars, even when locked.
● When driving, be aware of other cars who may flag you to pull over; it could be a ruse for robbery.
● Be particularly careful with belongings on beaches and in crowded tourist areas.

INSURANCE

Check your insurance coverage and buy a supplementary policy if necessary. EU nationals receive medical treatment with the European Health Insurance Card (EHIC). Obtain this card before travelling. Full health and travel insurance is still advised.

VISITORS WITH DISABILITIES

As in most parts of Spain, access is patchy. Major attractions such as the Alhambra and the Museo Picasso have been fully adapted for wheelchair use, while others have been in part or not at all. In general, historic buildings (particularly churches) and more remote beaches are very difficult. For further information see Turismo Polibea (www.polibea.com/turismo) and Accessible Andalucía (www.accessibleandalucia.com).

Getting Around

MAPS

City maps are available at all tourist offices or from the information desks at El Corte Inglés department stores in Granada, Málaga, Córdoba and Sevilla. A handy interactive map of the Costa del Sol can be found on the official tourist website of the region. See www.visitcostadelsol.com.

STRAIT ACROSS

Whilst the Costa del Sol's numerous marinas offer countless boat charters and rental, it is also possible to travel across the Strait of Gibraltar to northern Africa on the sea. Trasmediterranea's ferries sail overnight from Málaga across the strait to Melilla or from Algeceris to Tangier or Ceuta in a mere couple of hours, making crossing continents an enticing overnight excursion ☎ 902 45 46 45; www.trasmediterranea. es. High-speed catamarans make the journey even quicker. The company FRS has services from Tarifa to Tangier (35 minutes), from Algerciras (70 minutes) and from Gibraltar (80 minutes) ☎ 956 68 18 30; www.frs.es. In all cases note that you will need to take your passport if travelling to Tangier or Gibraltar and non-EU nationals should also check visa requirements.

BUSES

The Costa del Sol has an excellent bus network, which is generally the most common and efficient form of public transport to all parts of the region. Málaga's main bus station is located at the Paseo de Tilos, beside the Renfe railway station and about 15 minutes walk from the city centre. Buses servicing the western Costa del Sol are run by Autobuses Portillo (☎ 902 14 31 44; www.ctsa-portillo.com) with regular services to major destinations such as Mijas, Torremolinos, Marbella and Estepona. The eastern coast, as far as Almeria, is serviced by Alsina Graells (☎ 902 42 22 42; www.alsa.es) who also have regular buses to the provincial capitals of Sevilla, Granada and Córdoba.

BICYCLES

As in other Spanish cities, bicycle hire is becoming an increasingly popular way to see the sites. Málaga by Bike has city and mountain bikes for rent and offer cultural and coastal tours on two wheels (☎ 952 29 73 24; www.Malagabybike. com). If you are going to be in Sevilla for an extended period, consider subscribing to the city's Sevici bike share service. To do so, you will need to leave a deposit of €150 via a credit card, which is returned after 7 days. After that you can use one of their bikes free for the first 20 minutes and €1 per hour after that. You can subscribe via their website (www.sevici.es) or by calling ☎ 902 01 10 32 (both services in Spanish only). In other cities, your hotel should be able to advise you on where to hire a bike, or enquire at the tourist office.

TAXIS

Taxis are plentiful in the cities and towns, less so in remote villages where you may have to call for one in advance. Whilst in the urban centres they are obliged to turn on the meter; many taxis will go long distances along the coast for a fixed fee. For example a taxi from Málaga to Fuengirola should cost about €35, or €58 to Marbella. For fixed price trips, always ask

for the exact price before you set off.
Here are some reliable services:

- Sevilla: Teletaxi ☎ 954 62 22 22
- Málaga: Taxi Union ☎ 952 04 08 04
- Córdoba: Radio Taxi Córdoba ☎ 957 76 44 44
- Granada: Asociación Autónomos Taxis
  ☎ 958 28 06 54
- Jerez de la Frontera: Teletaxi ☎ 956 34 48 60

TRAINS

Train services are limited along the Costa. The only city to have a short distance train service is Málaga, which has two lines that travel westwards (along the coast) and northwards (to the interior). The C1 western-bound line is a relaxed way to reach the resort towns of Torremolinos, Benalmádena and Fuengirola, with trains leaving every 30 minutes. The C2 line is a picturesque journey to the main towns of the Guardalhorce Valley. There are also five daily trains to Sevilla and nine to Córdoba. All trains leave from the Renfe station on the Esplanada de la Estación, about 15 minutes walk from the city centre.

GUIDED WALKS

All tourist offices in Málaga and the regional capitals organize walking tours of the city, some with thematic or theatrical touches. For example, the Córdoba Tourist Board offers a nighttime tour of the principal sights, which includes short re-enactments of historical events and finishes with a drink and tapas in a typical tavern (☎ 902 20 17 74; www.turismodecordoba. org). If food is of more interest to you than history and monuments, try a tapas tour in Granada. The tour guides take you *tapeando* around the city's tapas hot spots whilst filling you in on local history and culture (☎ 619 44 49 84; www.granadatapastours.com). Unscrupulous guides are rare in Spain, and you would never be offered one through the tourist offices. However if you want to make sure, ask if your guide is a member of APIT, Spain's association of professional tourist guides.

HIKING

The interior of the Costa del Sol boasts some fabulous walking trails, and the close proximity of the region's famous *pueblos blancos* (white villages) ensure lots of places to rest up. The book *Walking in Andalucía* by Guy Hunter-Watts (Santana, ISBN 8489954550) details walks in all of Andalucía's natural parks. On the net see www.white-village.com for information on trails around the Ronda region or www.spanish-steps.com for a Málaga-based, husband-and-wife team who organize walking tours of the sierras.

Essential Facts

LOST AND FOUND

Municipal Lost Property Offices (Oficinas de Objectos Perdidos):
● Málaga: Calle Victoria 15 ☎ 952 32 72 00
● Sevilla: Calle Manuel Vazquez Sagastizabal 3 ☎ 954 42 04 03
● Granada: Pza. del Carmen s/n ☎ 958 24 81 03
● Jerez: Police Station, Avenida de la Comédia s/n ☎ 956 14 99 09

MONEY

The Euro (€) is the official currency of Spain. Banknotes are in official denominations of 5, 10, 20, 50, 100, 200 and 500 euros and coins in denominations of 1, 2, 5, 10, 20, 50 cents and 1 and 2 euros.

5 euros

10 euros

50 euros

100 euros

ELECTRICITY

● The standard current is 220 volts.
● Plugs are of the round two-pin type.

ETIQUETTE

● Spaniards rarely form linear queues, but are aware of their place in the service order by asking '¿quién es el último? (who is the last one?) on arrival.
● Smoking laws have become stricter over the past years. Most larger restaurants now have a non-smoking section and smoking is banned in public buildings and on public transport.
● When ordering in busy tapas bars you may have to shout to make yourself noticed.
● Niceties such as 'please' (por favor) and 'thank you' (gracias) are used more sparingly.
● When you meet someone of the opposite sex on a social level, it is customary to kiss them once on both cheeks.
● Tipping is discretionary. For a coffee and/or a snack, it is customary to round payment up to the nearest euro. For restaurants, between 5 and 10 per cent is sufficient.
● Drinks are normally tallied up and paid for before you leave, not after each round.
● As a sign of respect, cover shoulders, stomachs and thighs when visiting churches.

MAIL

● It's easier and quicker to buy stamps (sellos) from tobacconists (tabacs).
● To send large parcels and registered mail you will need to go to a post office (oficina de correos). Málaga's main post office is located at Avenida de Andalucía 1.
● Post boxes are yellow with two slots, one for Spain and the other for overseas (extranjero).

MEDIA

● The Costa del Sol's sizable foreign community has generated a lively English-language media scene. Radio, which generally has a mixture of news, chat and music includes Talk Radio Europe (91.9 FM in the west and 104.8 FM

in the east), Coastline Radio (97.6 FM) and Spectrum FM (105.5 FM). Onda Cero International (101.6 FM), part of a major Spanish network, is broadcast in various languages (including English) in and around Marbella. The BBC World Service can be picked up on short wave all over the region on differing frequencies.

● A host of free English language magazines can be picked up in pubs and restaurants. Newspapers include the expatriate targeted *Costa del Sol News* or the more serious *Sur* in English, an English language edition of Málaga's top selling daily *Diario Sur*.

MEDICAL AND HEALTHCARE

● Pharmacies (*farmacias*) are indicated by a flashing green cross; they are usually open 9.30–2 and 5–8. All post a list of *farmacias de guardia* (all-night chemists).

● Spanish pharmacists may be able to provide some medicines usually available only with a prescription in other countries.

MONEY MATTERS

● Most major travellers cheques can be changed at banks and/or bureaux de change.
● Credit (and debit) cards are accepted in all large establishments and many smaller ones. Note that you need to show some photo ID when making a purchase with a credit card.
● Multilingual ATM machines are everywhere in the larger towns. Even tiny villages will generally have one ATM machine.

NATIONAL HOLIDAYS

● 1 Jan, 6 Jan, Maundy Thursday (except Catalonia; Mar/Apr), Good Friday (Mar/Apr), 1 May, 15 Aug, 12 Oct, 1 Nov, 6 Dec, 8 Dec, 25 Dec (autonomous regions have their own additional holidays).

OPENING HOURS

● Banks: banks generally open from 8.30 to 2, Monday to Friday.
● Shops: smaller shops are open from 9.30/10

EMERGENCIES

● Police, Fire, Ambulance and all emergencies call: 112.
● Note that in the case of theft or loss, you must obtain a *denuncio* (official statement) from a police station for insurance and indemnity purposes.

TOURIST OFFICES

● Málaga: Avenida Cervantes 1 and Plaza Marina 11
☎ 952 12 20 20;
www.Malagaturismo.com
● Sevilla: Plaza del Triunfo, 1
☎ 954 21 00 05 and Plaza de San Francisco s/n
☎ 954 59 52 88;
www.turismosevilla.org
● Granada: Calle Virgen Blanca 9
☎ 902 40 50 45;
www.granadatur.com
● Córdoba: Calle Rey Heredía 22 (temporary address) and kiosk at Plaza de Tendillas 4
☎ 902 20 17 74;
www.turismodecordoba.org
● Jerez de la Frontera: Alameda Cristina (Edificio Los Claustros)
☎ 956 34 17 11;
www.turismojerez.com

to 1.30/2 then again from 4/4.30 to 8/8.30, Monday to Saturday. Larger shops, especially if located in the city centres, forgo the midday closing and stay open all day. Sunday trading is restricted to shops selling food, and to tourist-targeted retailers.

● Museums: most major museums close Monday and Sunday afternoons. Many smaller ones open mornings only.

● Restaurants: restaurant kitchens catering to locals will rarely open before 8.30pm, though it's easy to have an early meal in the resorts and touristy areas. Some fashionable restaurants may open all day—part of a new trend in Spain.

TELEPHONES

● Public telephones take both coins and *tarjetas*, Telefónica (Spain's major phone provider) telephone cards that can be bought from news stands.

● It's often easier to use a *locutorio* for long distance calls. *Locutorios* are cut-price call centres where you make calls from a private phone booth. Many also offer internet and fax services.

● Phone cards are another cheap way to make long distance calls. These are offered by a number of providers and are available from *locutorios* and convenience shops. A €6-card will allow you several hours of long distance calling time when used from a land line.

● Spain uses the GSM mobile phone system, which is compatible with most mobile phones except those from the USA. If your phone is uncoded (ie is not 'locked' into one provider) you can buy a 'pay as you go' SIM card and use it with a local provider on local rates. If not, you will pay roaming rates.

● To call Spain from the UK dial 00 34 followed by the local number. To call the UK from Spain dial 00 44, to Australia 00 61 and the USA 00 1.

TOILETS

● Popular beaches have portaloos. Bars generally let you use their facilities, though it's polite to buy a drink at the bar as well.

Language

With tourism being a major industry, English (and to a lesser extent German and French) is common along the coast. Making yourself understood will not be difficult here, but more so inland in the villages. Even for those who have a handle on the language the lisping, southern Spanish accent will be quite a challenge, but of course any efforts will always be much appreciated.

BASIC VOCABULARY

yes/no	*si/no*
I don't understand	*no entiendo*
I don't speak Spanish	*no hablo español*
left/right	*izquierda/derecha*
entrance/exit	*entrada/salida*
open/closed	*abierto/cerrado*
good/bad	*bueno/malo*
big/small	*grande/pequeño*
with/without	*con/sin*
more/less	*más/menos*
hot/cold	*caliente/frio*
early/late	*temprano/tarde*
here/there	*aquí/alli*
today/tomorrow/	*hoy/mañana*
yesterday	*ayer*
how much is it...?	*¿cuénto es?*
where is the ...?	*¿donde está....*
do you have...?	*¿tiene...?*
I'd like...	*me gustaría*

EATING OUT

menu	*la carta*
glass of wine	*copa de vino*
glass of beer	*caña*
water (mineral)	*agua (mineral)*
still/sparkling	*sin gas/con gas*
coffee (with milk)	*café (con leche)*
May I have the bill?	*La cuenta, por favor*
Do you take credit cards?	*¿Aceptan tarjetas de crédito?*
set dishes	*platos combinados*
smoking allowed	*se permite fumar*
no smoking	*se prohibe fumar*

NUMBERS

1	*uno*
2	*dos*
3	*tres*
4	*cuatro*
5	*cinco*
6	*seis*
7	*siete*
8	*ocho*
9	*nueve*
10	*diez*
11	*once*
12	*doce*
13	*trece*
14	*catorce*
15	*quince*
16	*dieciséis*
17	*diecisiete*
18	*dieciocho*
19	*diecinueve*
20	*veinte*
30	*treinta*
40	*cuarenta*
50	*cincuenta*
60	*sesanta*
70	*setanta*
80	*ochenta*
90	*noventa*
100	*cien*
1000	*mil*

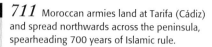

Timeline

BEFORE AD700

Southern Spain becomes the domain of the Roman empire by 27BC, Latin becomes the root of the Spanish language and Córdoba is established as the capital. As the empire declines in the 4th century, tribes from Northern Europe move in and occupy the region for over 300 years before the Moorish invasion and the birth of Al-Andalus.

711 Moroccan armies land at Tarifa (Cádiz) and spread northwards across the peninsula, spearheading 700 years of Islamic rule.

930 Córdoba, by now the capital of Andalus (Moorish Andalucía), becomes a renowned centre of study, culture and trade.

1031 Al-Andalus fragments into separate states. Christian forces from the north attack and occupy Moorish territory.

1212 King Alfonso VIII begins the Reconquista (re-conquering) of Al-Andalus.

1236 Córdoba's famous mosque is converted to a cathedral.

1487 Málaga falls to Christian forces. Five years later King Boabdil hands the keys of Granada to the Catholic rulers and evacuates the Alhambra.

1570 Sevilla prospers from the wealth of the conquistadores returning from the Americas.

1599 Diego Velázquez is born in Sevilla.

1620 Coffers are squandered by dysfunctional Christian rulers. Plague and poverty spread throughout the region.

1704 The British Empire lays claim to Gibraltar.

From left: the impressive mosque in Córdoba; a statue of artist Velázquez who was born in Sevilla; detail of the Palacios Nazaries at the Alhambra, Granada; façade of the Monasterio de la Cartuja, Granada; the glitzy resort of Puerto Banús

1805 The Spanish Armada is defeated in the Battle of Trafalgar off the coast of Cádiz. Left-wing radicalism takes hold of southern Spain.

1898 George Langworthy ('El Inglés') converts a castle in Torremolinos into a hotel. Tourism along the coast is born.

1929 Sevilla hosts the world Expo. The term 'Costa del Sol' first appears.

1931 The Second Republic is declared.

1936 The left-wing Popular Front wins the elections. General Franco launches a nationalist uprising, plunging the country into civil war. Famed writer and poet Federico García Lorca is shot by fascist troops near Granada.

1954 The Marbella Club is founded and the town starts to attract the international jet set.

1960s–70s Costa del Sol tourism booms.

1975 General Franco dies. Democratic elections follow.

1992 Sevilla hosts its second Expo; the high speed AVE train connects the city with Madrid.

2007 Representatives of Spain's Islamic community unsuccessfully petition the Catholic church to be allowed to once again worship in Córdoba's mosque.

MÁLAGA PEOPLE

● Pablo Ruiz Picasso (1881–1973) is perhaps the most famous Malagueño of all. He was born in the city at number 36 Plaza de Riego (now called Plaza de la Merced) to a father who was an art teacher. When he was 14, the family moved north; first to La Coruña and then Barcelona. Pablo never returned to Málaga but many critics see an influence of the Costa's special light in his early work.

● Javier Conde (b1975) is a famous bullfighter. In 1995 he took the *alternativa* (elevating him to the status of toreador) in Málaga's bull-ring La Malagueta. In 2001 he married the flamenco artist Estrella Morente.

Index

TWINPACK
Costa del Sol

WRITTEN BY Mary-Ann Gallagher
VERIFIED BY Mona Kraus and Lindsay Bennett
COVER DESIGN Jacqueline Bailey
DESIGN WORK Jacqueline Bailey and Maggie Aldred
INDEXER Marie Lorimer
IMAGE RETOUCHING AND REPRO Sarah Montgomery, Michael Moody and James Tims
PROJECT EDITOR Apostrophe S Limited
SERIES EDITOR Cathy Harrison

© **AA MEDIA LIMITED 2010**

Colour separation by AA Digital Department
Printed and bound by Leo Paper Products, China

A CIP catalogue record for this book is available from the British Library.

ISBN 978-0-7495-6149-9

Published by AA Publishing, a trading name of AA Media Limited, whose registered office is Fanum House, Basing View, Basingstoke, Hampshire RG21 4EA. Registered number 06112600.

Front cover image: AA/P Wilson
Back cover images: (i) AA/J Edmanson; (ii) AA/C Sawyer; (iii) AA/A Molyneux; (iv) AA/D Robertson

A03639
Maps in this title produced from map data supplied by Global Mapping, Brackley, UK. Copyright © Global Mapping/Rugoma

The Automobile Association would like to thank the following photographers, companies and picture libraries for their assistance in the preparation of this book.

Abbreviations for the pictures credits are as follows – (t) top; (b) bottom; (c) centre; (l) left; (r) right; (AA) AA World Travel Library.

1 AA/J Tims; 2–18 top panel AA/A Molyneux; 4 AA/J Edmanson; 5 AA/D Robertson; 6tl AA/M Chaplow; 6tc AA/P Wilson; 6tr AA/A Molyneux; 6bl Bleda y Rosa/Museo Picasso Málaga; 6bc AA/M Chaplow; 6br AA/C Sawyer; 7tl AA/P Wilson; 7tc AA/J Edmanson; 7tr AA/J Edmanson; 7bl AA/J Edmanson; 7bc AA/P Wilson; 10t AA/S McBride; 10c(i) AA/M Chaplow; 10c(ii) AA/M Chaplow; 10b AA/D Robertson; 11t(i) AA/M Chaplow; 11t(ii) AA/M Chaplow; 11c AA/M Chaplow; 11b AA/J Edmanson; 12t AA/J Tims; 12c(i) AA/J Poulsen; 12c(ii) AA/J Poulsen; 12b AA/C Sawyer; 13t(i) AA/C Sawyer; 13t(ii) AA/M Chaplow; 13c AA/D Robertson; 13b AA/A Molyneux; 14t AA/A Molyneux; 14c(i) AA/M Chaplow; 14c(ii) AA/A Molyneux; 14b AA/S McBride; 16t AA/M Chaplow; 16c(i) AA/M Chaplow; 16c(ii) AA/J Tims; 16b AA/D Robertson; 17t AA/A Molyneux; 17c(i) AA/M Chaplow; 17c(ii) AA/M Chaplow; 17b AA/J Tims; 18t AA/P Benett; 18c AA/C Sawyer; 18b AA/D Robertson; 19t AA/J Tims; 19c AA/M Chaplow; 19b AA/J Tims; 20–21 AA/M Chaplow; 24l AA/M Chaplow; 24c AA/J Poulsen; 24r AA/P Wilson; 25l AA/P Wilson; 25r AA/P Wilson; 26 Bleda y Rosa/Museo Picasso Málaga; 27 Bleda y Rosa/Museo Picasso Málaga; 28–30 top panel AA/M Chaplow; 28l AA/J Edmanson; 28r AA/M Chaplow; 29l Centro de Arte Contemporáneo de Malaga; 29r AA/J Poulsen; 30l AA/D Robertson; 30r AA/J Tims; 31 AA/M Chaplow; 32–33 top panel AA/D Robertson; 34–35 AA/J Tims; 36–38 AA/C Sawyer; 39 AA/J Tims; 42l AA/P Wilson; 42r AA/D Robertson; 43l AA/M Chaplow; 43r AA/M Chaplow; 44 AA/M Chaplow; 44/45t AA/M Chaplow; 44br AA/M Chaplow; 45l AA/M Chaplow; 45r AA/J Edmanson; 46l John Glover/Alamy; 46r Keith Shuttlewood/Alamy; 47l AA/M Chaplow; 47r AA/D Robertson; 48t AA/P Wilson; 48bl AA/P Wilson; 48br AA/M Chaplow; 49tl AA/J Edmanson; 49r AA/M Jourdan; 49br AA/P Wilson; 50l AA/M Chaplow; 50tr AA/J Tims; 50br AA/M Chaplow; 51t AA/M Chaplow; 51b AA/J Tims; 52l AA/M Chaplow; 52r AA/M Chaplow; 53l AA/J Edmanson; 53r AA/J Tims; 54l AA/D Robertson; 54tr AA/W Voysey; 54br AA/P Wilson; 55t AA/J Poulsen; 55b AA/W Voysey; 56l AA/J Edmanson; 56r AA/A Molyneux; 57l AA/A Molyneux; 57r AA/P Wilson; 58t AA/P Wilson; 58bl AA/A Molyneux; 58br AA/M Chaplow; 58/59 AA/A Molyneux; 59 AA/J Edmanson; 60l AA/A Molyneux; 60tr AA/A Molyneux; 60br AA/J Edmanson; 61t AA/P Wilson; 61bl AA/J Edmanson; 61br AA/A Molyneux; 62l AA/J Edmanson; 62r AA/P Wilson; 63–67 top panel AA/J Edmanson; 63l AA/M Chaplow; 63r AA/J Edmanson; 64l AA/D Robertson; 64r AA/M Chaplow; 65 AA/J Tims; 66l AA/P Wilson; 66r AA/M Chaplow; 67l AA/J Edmanson; 67r AA/D Robertson; 68 AA/M Chaplow; 69 AA/M Chaplow; 70–71 AA/D Robertson; 72–73 AA/J Tims; 74–78 AA/C Sawyer; 77 AA/D Robertson; 79 AA/J Edmanson; 82l AA/J Tims; 82r AA/J Tims; 83l AA/M Chaplow; 83r AA/M Chaplow; 84 AA/M Chaplow; 85 AA/M Chaplow; 86t AA/J Edmanson; 86bl AA/J Edmanson; 86bc AA/J Edmanson; 86br AA/M Chaplow; 87 AA/D Robertson; 88 AA/J Tims; 89 AA/J Tims; 90l AA/J Tims; 90r AA/M Chaplow; 91 AA/J Tims; 92l Jose Manuel Revuelta Luna/Alamy; 92r Jose Manuel Revuelta Luna/AlAA/Alamy; 93l AA/J Tims; 93r AA/D Robertson; 94–97 top panel AA/J Poulsen; 94l AA/D Robertson; 94r AA/M Chaplow; 95 Mark Alexander/Alamy; 96l Parque de las Ciencias, Andalucia–Granada; 96r AA/P Enticknap; 97l AA/J Tims; 97r AA/J Tims; 98 AA/M Chaplow; 99–100 AA/D Robertson; 101–102 AA/J Tims; 103–106 AA/C Sawyer; 104 AA/D Robertson; 107 AA/J Tims; 108–112 top panel AA/C Sawyer; 108t La Botica de Vejer; 108c(i) Hotel Amadeus Sevilla; 108c(ii) Hotel Amadeus Sevilla; 108b Hotel Casa del Conde de Pinofiel; 113 AA/A Molyneux; 114–125 top panel AA/C Sawyer; 119 AA/C Sawyer; 120 MRI Bankers' Guide to Foreign Currency, Houston, USA; 122t AA/P Baker; 122c AA/C Sawyer; 122b AA/J Tims; 124l AA/J Edmanson; 124c AA/M Jourdan; 124r AA/M Chaplow; 125l AA/A Molyneux; 125r AA/J Poulsen.

Every effort has been made to trace the copyright holders, and we apologise in advance for any accidental errors. We would be happy to apply any corrections in the following edition of this publication.